STARTING AND OPERATING LIVE VIRTUAL REFERENCE SERVICES

A How-To-Do-It Manual for Librarians

Marc Meola
Sam Stormont

HOW-TO-DO-IT MANUALS FOR LIBRARIANS

NUMBER 118

NEAL-SCHUMAN PUBLISHERS, INC.
New York, London

Published by Neal-Schuman Publishers, Inc.
100 Varick Street
New York, NY 10013

Copyright © 2002 by Marc Meola and Sam Stormont

All rights reserved. Reproduction of this book, in whole or in part, without written permission of the publisher, is prohibited.

Printed and bound in the United States of America.

The paper used in this publication meets the minimum requirements of American National Standard for Information Sciences—Permanence of Paper for Printed Library Materials, ANSI Z39.48–1992 ∞

Library of Congress Cataloging-in-Publication Data

Meola, Marc, 1968-
   Starting and operating live virtual reference services: a how-to-do-it manual for libarians/Marc Meola and Sam Stormont.
     p. cm. — (How-to-do-it manuals for librarians; no. 118)
   Includes bibliographical references and index.
   ISBN 1-55570-444-1 (alk. paper)
   1. Internet in Library reference services. 2. Electronic reference service (Libraries). I. Stormont, Sam, II. Title. III. How-to-do-it manuals for libraries; no. 118.
   Z711.47 .M46 2002
   025.524—dc21

2002005808

CONTENTS

List of Figures — ix

Preface — xi

Part I. Understanding the Essentials of Live Virtual Reference

1. Understanding Live Virtual Reference — 3
   - Live Virtual Reference Defined — 3
   - Live Virtual Reference Compared to Other Forms of Reference — 8
     - Face-to-Face In-Person Desk Reference — 9
     - Telephone Reference — 10
     - E-Mail Virtual Reference — 10
     - 24/7 Reference — 11
     - Collaborative Reference — 12
     - Ask-A Reference — 12
     - Remote Patron Reference — 12
   - What Is Live Virtual Reference Called? — 13
   - Summary — 15
   - References — 15

2. Offering Live Virtual Reference — 17
   - Ten Reasons to Offer Live Virtual Reference — 17
     - Serve Users Where They Are Searching — 17
     - Keep Up with Rising Expectations — 18
     - Answer Questions with Faster Response Time — 18
     - Conduct Virtual Reference Interviews — 19
     - Show Instead of Tell — 19
     - Serve Distance Learners — 19
     - Connect with the New Generation — 20
     - Empower Users with Differing Abilities — 20
     - Create Excitement and Learn Cutting-Edge Skills — 20
     - Pursue Marketing and Relationship Building — 21
   - Ten Obstacles to Overcome When Offering Live Virtual Reference — 22

	Coping with Additional Workload	22
	Generating Initial and Continued Support	22
	Finding Qualified Technical Personnel	23
	Controlling Costs and Getting Funding	23
	Re-envisioning Your Library as a Virtual Place	23
	Dispelling Fear of the Unknown	24
	Recognizing Limitations to Text-Based Chat	24
	Working with Cranky Library Faculty	25
	Trouble-Shooting Sundry Technical Headaches	25
	Understanding Copyright and Renegotiating Licenses	26
	Summary	26
	References	27
3.	Exploring the Five Models of Live Virtual Reference	29
	Basic Model—Free or Low Cost Chat	29
	Homegrown Model—Create or Download Open Source Software	32
	Advanced Model—Sophisticated Software, Single Institution	36
	Collaborative Model—Working with Other Libraries	40
	Corporate Call Center Model—Staffing for Efficiency and Profit	45
	Summary	51
	References	52

Part II. Preparing for Live Virtual Reference

4.	Planning for Live Virtual Reference—A Nine-Step Process	55
	Step 1: Articulate a Vision	55
	Step 2: Form a Committee	57
	Step 3: Gather Information	59
	Step 4: Investigate Funding	59
	Step 5: Decide on Staffing	60
	Step 6: Select Software	60
	Step 7: Draft Policy	61
	Audience	61
	Level of Service	61
	Privacy	62

	Step 8: Implement Live Virtual Reference	63
	Step 9: Evaluate Live Virtual Reference	64
	Summary	65
	References	65
5.	Gathering Information on Live Virtual Reference	67
	Explore the External Environment	67
	Web Pages	67
	Surveys	70
	Listservs	72
	Telephone Interviews	72
	Bibliographies	72
	Conferences	73
	Assess the Internal Environment	73
	Consider Your Institutional or Community Framework	74
	Examine Your Library Environment	75
	Consider Your Reference Department	76
	Summary	78
	References	78
6.	Deciding on a Staffing Model for Live Virtual Reference	79
	Choose the Basic Staffing Model	79
	Advantages of Basic Staffing Model	80
	Disadvantages of Basic Staffing Model	80
	Implement the Homegrown Staffing Model	82
	Adopt the Advanced Staffing Model	83
	Problems with the Advanced Staffing Model and Their Solutions	83
	Hours of the Advanced Staffing Model	84
	Who Answers Questions in the Advanced Staffing Model	84
	Where Are Questions Answered in the Advanced Staffing Model	85
	Participate in the Collaborative Staffing Model	86
	Beware of the Corporate Staffing Model	88
	Summary	89
	References	89

7. Selecting Software for Live Virtual Reference—Five Options 91
    Put Software in Perspective 91
    Involve Your Systems Staff 93
    Ask These Questions About Software 96
    Option 1: Use Basic Software 96
        AOL Instant Messenger 97
        LivePerson 98
    Option 2: Grow Your Own Homegrown Software 100
        Temple University 101
        Miami University 102
        Southern Illinois University 103
    Option 3: Pay for Advanced Software 105
        LSSI 107
        24/7 Reference 108
    Option 4: Share Costs with Collaborative Software 110
    Option 5: Monitor Corporate Software Developments 111
    Summary 113
    References 113

Part III. Implementing and Incorporating Live Virtual Reference

8. Training the Staff for Live Virtual Reference 117
    General Skills for All Models 117
        Core Reference Skills 118
        Real-Time Chat Techniques 119
        Software Specific Skills 122
        Live Virtual Reference Policies 122
    Training for the Basic Model 123
    Training for the Homegrown Model 124
    Training for the Advanced Model. 125
    Training for the Collaborative Model 126
    Training for the Corporate Model 128
    Summary 129
    References 130

9. Marketing for Live Virtual Reference 131
    Marketing the Basic Model 134

Marketing the Homegrown Model	136
Marketing the Advanced Model	137
Marketing the Collaborative Model	139
Marketing the Corporate Model	141
Summary	143
References	144

10. Evaluating Your Live Virtual Reference 145
    Process for Evaluating All Models 145
        Revisit Your Vision 146
        Evaluate Software 146
        Assess Staffing 147
        Review Questions 148
        Analyze Answers 149
        Produce a Report 150
    Evaluating the Basic Model 150
    Evaluating the Homegrown Model 152
    Evaluating the Advanced Model 153
    Evaluating the Collaborative Model 155
    Evaluating the Corporate Model 156
    Summary 157
    References 157

Glossary 159

Index 163

About the Authors 167

LIST OF FIGURES

Figure 1–1: Example of a patron submitting a live virtual question. Used with permission. — 5

Figure 1–2: Librarian side of live virtual reference interaction. Used with permission. — 6

Figure 1–3: Patron response: "Ok, I can hold." Used with permission. — 7

Figure 1–4: End of a live virtual reference interaction. Used with permission. — 8

Figure 3–1: SUNY Morrisville home page home page before clicking on Talk to a Librarian Live! link. Used with permission. — 30

Figure 3–2: SUNY Morrisville home page after clicking on Talk to a Librarian Live! link. Used with permission. — 31

Figure 3–3: Miami University Ask a Question Web page. Used with permission. — 34

Figure 3–4: Miami University Live Online Assistance form. Used with permission. — 35

Figure 3–5: Miami University text message from a librarian. Used with permission. — 36

Figure 3–6: Example of Miami University live transaction. Used with permission. — 37

Figure 3–7: Miami University logout screen. Used with permission. — 38

Figure 3–8: North Carolina State University Ask A Librarian Live. Used with permission. — 39

Figure 3–9: NCSU example of page pushing: Directions to the library. Used with permission. — 40

Figure 3–10: NCSU summary of links at end of transaction. Used with permission. — 41

Figure 3–11: Q and A NJ patron submitting a question. Used with permission. — 42

Figure 3–12: Q and A NJ patron receives Web site pushed by librarian. Used with permission. — 43

Figure 3–13: Q and A NJ patron receives summary of links pushed by librarian. Used with permission. — 44

Figure 3–14: Lands' End Contact Us Web page. Used with permission. — 45

Figure 3–15: Lands' End providing phone or chat option. Used with permission. 46

Figure 3–16: Text chat window: "Welcome to Lands' End Live!" Used with permission. 47

Figure 3–17: Lands' End chat box and page push. Used with permission. 48

Figure. 3–18: Lands' End "Thank you for participating" Web page. Used with permission. 49

Figure 5–1: LiveRef(sm): A Registry of Real-time Digital Reference Services. Used with permission. 68

Figure 5–2: Homepage of the Teaching Librarian. Used with permission. 70

Figure 5–3: Carnegie Mellon Survey of Chat Reference Service. Used with permission. 71

Figure 7–1: AOL IM at SUNY Morrisville. Used with permission. 98

Figure 7–2: LivePerson at University of Tennessee Libraries. Used with permission. 99

Figure 7–3: Temple TalkNow Homegrown software. Used with permission. 102

Figure 7–4: Miami Univeristy (Ohio) Rakim homegrown software. Used with permission. 103

Figure 7–5: LSSI software as used at NCSU Libraries. Used with permission. 107

Figure 7–6: Santa Monica Public Library using 24/7 software. Used with permission. 109

Figure 7–7: Collaborative software as used by Q & A NJ. Used with permission. 111

PREFACE

Starting and Operating Live Virtual Reference Services offers a blueprint to help your library join the hundreds of libraries that now offer live virtual reference—an exciting new way to reach library users in real-time through the World Wide Web. Our goal is to help those who are new to live virtual reference learn how to build a live virtual reference service from the ground up; those already offering live virtual reference will learn how to evaluate their current service and compare it to the different types of services now being offered.

We start with the basics and explain what live virtual reference is, why you should offer it, and how to choose the best model of live virtual reference for your library. Then we take you step-by-step through the planning process and guide you through difficult decisions such as choosing a staffing model and selecting software. Finally, we'll show you how to train your staff, market your service, and then evaluate it once it's up and running. From beginning to end, from thinking about live virtual reference to actually doing it, *Starting and Operating Live Virtual Reference Services* is your practical guide to starting and operating live virtual reference services.

The time is right for a practical manual on live virtual reference. Enough libraries are providing this service to confirm that it's not a passing fad, and a set of best practices from these libraries is now emerging. Still, many librarians are confused about live virtual reference and how to set it up in their libraries. We knew from conferences and listserv discussions that there were a lot of unanswered questions out there. We wrote this book to de-mystify live virtual reference and to codify the collective wisdom of practicing live virtual reference librarians. We describe our own experience as live virtual reference practitioners and the methods and approaches many virtual pioneers have found most effective.

The varied experiences of live virtual reference librarians show that there is more than one way to provide live reference: what's right for one library may not be right for yours. We present live virtual reference service in terms of five models—basic, homegrown, advanced, collaborative, and corporate. With this book you will be able to make informed, intelligent decisions as to the best model for your library.

Starting and Operating Live Virtual Reference Services is organized into three parts: Part I "Understanding the Essentials of Live Virtual Reference," Part II "Preparing for Live Virtual Reference," and Part III "Implementing and Incorporating Live Virtual Reference." Throughout the three parts we use five models of live virtual reference to organize the information we present—models we designate as *basic, homegrown, advanced, collaborative,* and *corporate.* The answers to questions about software, staffing, training, marketing, and evaluating are provided through the lens of the five models. We take you one step at a time through the entire process, but since each chapter focuses on a particular facet of live virtual reference, it is also possible to skip back and forth or go directly to a chapter discussing a specific aspect of the project.

Chapter 1, "Understanding Live Virtual Reference," lays out exactly what live virtual reference is, what it looks like, and how it compares to other forms of reference. We discuss how live virtual reference is similar to and differs from face-to-face in-person reference, telephone reference, e-mail virtual reference, 24/7 reference, collaborative reference, Ask-A reference, and remote patron reference. We then sort out the numerous terms that are often used to refer to live virtual reference so you can understand what everyone's talking about when they talk about virtual reference.

Chapter 2, "Offering Live Virtual Reference," presents ten reasons to offer live virtual reference and ten obstacles to overcome in offering live virtual reference. Use these reasons to make convincing arguments to yourself or to your colleagues. Be aware of the obstacles too, so you go in with your eyes wide open. The chapter concludes with a decision making worksheet to help you decide if live virtual reference is right for your institution.

The last chapter in this section, Chapter 3, "Exploring the Five Models of Live Virtual Reference," introduces the five models of live virtual reference—basic, homegrown, advanced, collaborative, and corporate. We explain the philosophies, staffing arrangements, software used, and show you what sample reference transactions look like in each model. Choose the model that best fits your library, mix and match to create a hybrid model, or get ideas to create an entirely new model.

After reading about the essentials in Part I, you will be ready to proceed to preparing for live virtual reference in Part II. Chapter 4, "Planning for Live Reference—A Nine-Step Process," presents an overview of the entire planning process and includes sections on articulating a vision, forming a committee, investigating funding, and drafting policy. Chapters 5, 6, and 7 go into more detail on the important planning steps of gathering information, deciding on staffing, and selecting software. The chapters in this section bring you to the point where you can start implementing a live virtual reference service.

In Part III, "Implementing and Incorporating Live Virtual Reference," the final three chapters cover training, marketing, and evaluating. In Chapter 8, "Training the Staff for Live Virtual Reference," we discuss the training your librarians will need to answer live virtual reference questions, including the core reference skills that must be adapted to the virtual environment as well as the new real-time techniques that apply specifically to chatting on the Internet. The differences in training techniques that are needed in the five different models of live virtual reference are presented and compared.

Chapter 9, "Marketing for Live Virtual Reference," explains the importance of marketing a live virtual reference service, a concept that may be new to some librarians. Practical tips and concrete suggestions are provided for each of the models. Chapter 10, "Evaluating Your Live Virtual Reference," completes the book and brings everything full circle: you revisit your vision, evaluate the software you have chosen, assess your staffing, review and analyze questions and answers, and produce a report that will tell your library where to go next with live virtual reference.

We all know the world is changing. *Starting and Operating Live Virtual Reference Services* is designed to help you deal with that change, by building a bridge from the traditional world of face-to-face reference to the real-time world of live virtual reference on the Internet.

ACKNOWLEDGMENTS

We would like to thank our colleagues at Temple University and the College of New Jersey. Special thanks go to participants of the listservs DIG-REF and Livereference, and to all the librarians who gave us permission to use screen shots of their services and generously shared their experiences. Michael Kelley, our editor at Neal-Schuman, kept us on schedule and provided comments that greatly improved the text. The College of New Jersey provided generous academic leave; without it this book could not have been written. We would like to especially thank our families—Andre, Caitlin, Colin and Christine—and all our friends for their understanding, support, and encouragement.

PART I

UNDERSTANDING THE ESSENTIALS OF LIVE VIRTUAL REFERENCE

1 UNDERSTANDING LIVE VIRTUAL REFERENCE

LIVE VIRTUAL REFERENCE DEFINED

Live virtual reference is the application of a new technology to a familiar library service. The new technology is the real-time communication power of the Internet; the familiar library service is traditional reference: providing high-quality, one-on-one human help to library users in search of information. Think of live virtual reference like vintage wine in a brand new bottle—providing human help to library users is the vintage wine, the Internet is the new bottle.

Just as face-to-face desk reference is the question answering service of the print-based library, virtual reference is the question answering service of the Web-based virtual library. A virtual library is incomplete without a virtual reference service. Until recently, librarians relied almost exclusively on asynchronous electronic mail to deliver virtual reference service. In the past five years, however, librarians have begun to use software that permits librarians and patrons to communicate "live," synchronously, in real-time. Live virtual reference is virtual reference that uses chat or text-messaging to communicate in real-time. Live virtual reference is the latest attempt to move to a closer simulation of traditional face-to-face reference for users who are increasingly virtual and not physically present in the physical library.

Live virtual reference, then, is *real-time human help delivered through the Internet*. Let's unpack this idea. Live virtual reference is *real-time*. What does real-time mean? Real-time means that users get their questions answered instantaneously, as they ask them, rather than having to wait up to 24 hours or longer as in e-mail virtual reference services. Real-time communication is synchronous, like telephone or in-person reference. Real-time is not asynchronous, like e-mail reference. Real-time is just a fancy way of saying the communication takes place *now*, with no in-between waiting period. The real-time or live aspect of live virtual reference is one of its most important distinguishing features. Why? Because real-time brings live virtual reference closer to the ideal of face-to-face reference for remote patrons: it facilitates virtual reference interviews and it speeds up response time. Real-time is what distinguishes live virtual reference from e-mail virtual reference.

Live virtual reference is *human help*. Human means users receive one-on-one assistance from real live human beings: not Web page help, not frequently asked question lists, not digital pathfinders, not automated answer bots, not expert systems. One-on-one personal service through human help is a core value of reference librarianship (Green 1876; Gorman 2001). As many have pointed out, the human help provided through live virtual reference is high tech; but at the same time high touch. Just because live virtual reference takes place through new technology, this doesn't necessarily mean that live virtual reference is "totally revolutionary," "the end of reference as we know it," "devoid of human values," "a de-skilled or de-professionalized version of reference" or somehow "evil" in any other way just because it's connected to a new technology. Live virtual reference maintains the human connection in the reference transaction.

Human help is mediation or assistance that can occur on a number of levels including directions and general information, technical assistance, information lookup, research consultation, and library instruction (Whitson, 1995). At almost every conference session on live virtual reference, someone always asks what kinds of questions are received in this kind of service. The answer is that the mix of live virtual questions very often mirrors the mix of questions a library receives at its physical reference desk. As Coffman and McGlamery have pointed out, the popularity of services such as Ask Jeeves (www.askjeeves.com) is evidence that patrons still need help locating information resources in a virtual environment (Coffman and McGlamery 2000). The way to deliver that help, however, has changed.

Live virtual reference is *delivered through the Internet*. A link from your library's home page enables librarians and users to communicate through Web-based text messaging and with some software packages to share Web pages by pushing and co-browsing. Let's look at a simulated example of live virtual reference. While searching for labor statistics on the Internet, a user tries to find help at your library's Web site. They connect to your library's Web page. They become confused and need help because they cannot find the information. They click on your live reference link. Up pops a Web form in which they submit a question (see Figure 1–1).

On the librarian side, an audio cue (like the chime that alerts you that a new e-mail has arrived) goes off telling you that a virtual reference user wants to ask a question. Up pops a window (see Figure 1–2).

The screen is split into two segments. The bottom portion is a record of the conversation, the top box is the place to type in

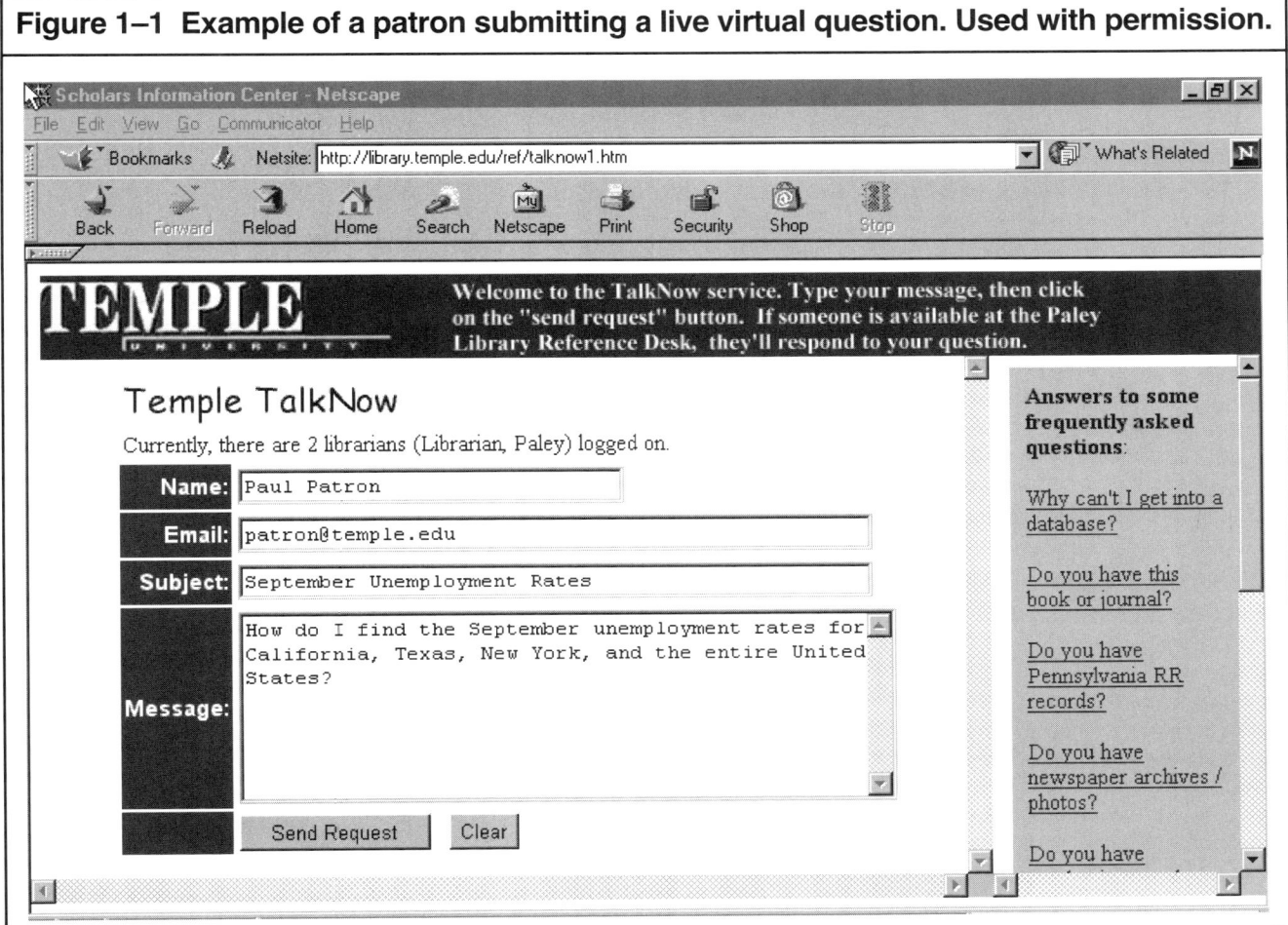

Figure 1–1 Example of a patron submitting a live virtual question. Used with permission.

messages. On the right is the patron's name, e-mail address, IP address, date and time, and a menu of canned responses. Canned responses are scripted messages such as "Hello, how can I help you" that can be used over and over again. The patron's question "How do I find the September unemployment rates for…appears above the system message which greets the patron on arrival. The librarian types in the message, "this might take a few minutes…would you like to hold." And then the patron replies, "Ok, I can hold," as in Figure 1–3.

In Figure 1–4, the librarian has sent the patron URLs for the data on unemployment from the Bureau of Labor Statistics. The patron is blown away at the librarian's skills and amazed that the library offers such a great service.

This particular example is based on Temple University's TalkNow service. This is an example of the homegrown model

6 STARTING AND OPERATING LIVE VIRTUAL REFERENCE SERVICES

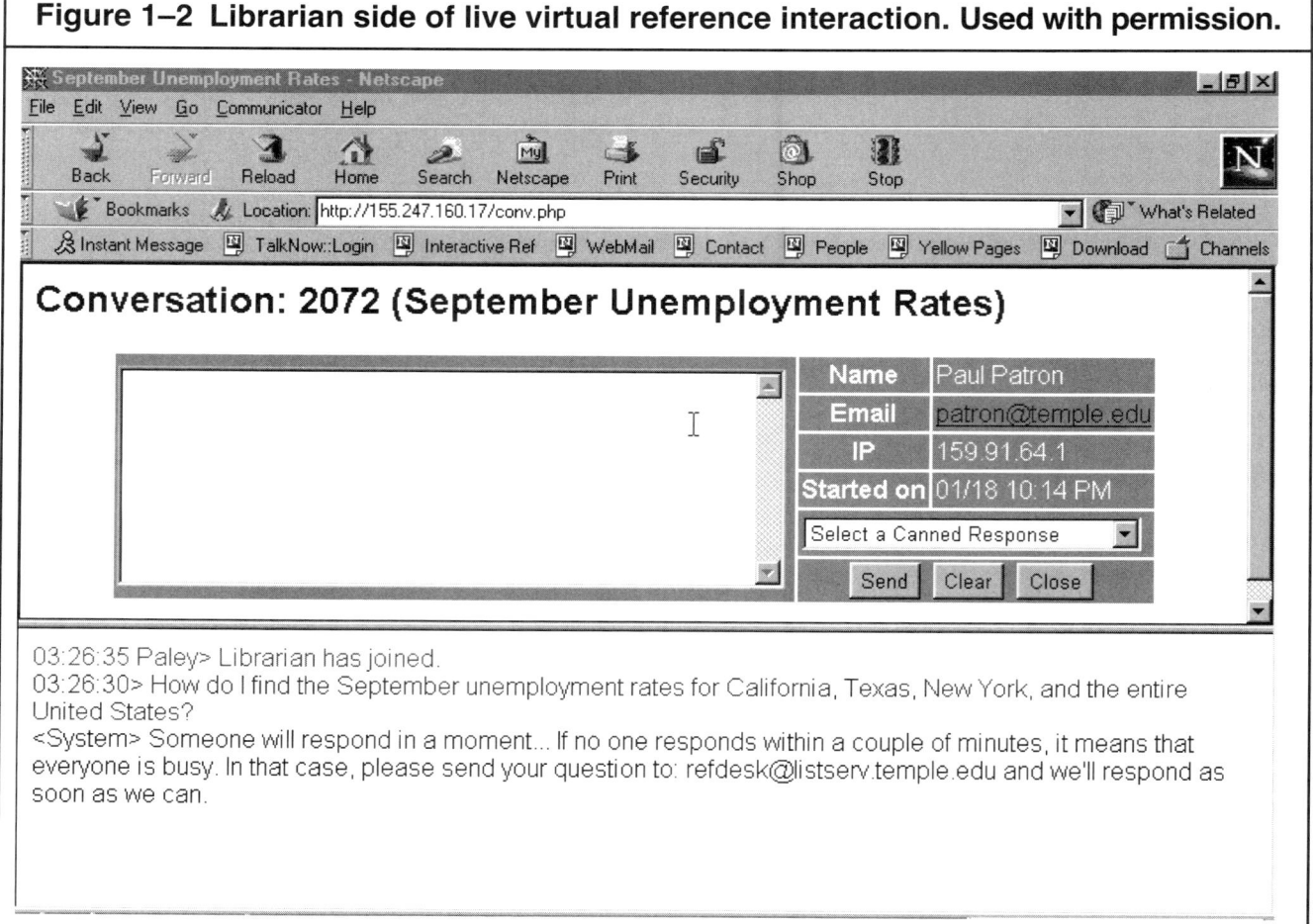

Figure 1–2 Librarian side of live virtual reference interaction. Used with permission.

of live virtual reference, described more fully in Chapter 3. In this example, page pushing (sending Web pages to the user's browser) or co-browsing (taking remote control of the user's browser) would have been very useful. If the software permitted page pushing, the librarian could have sent the Bureau of Labor Statistics Web page out to the patron's browser, instead of the librarian and patron having to cut and paste URLs. If the software had co-browsing, the librarian and user could take turns escorting each other to Web pages through the remote control of each other's browsers. These features are part of a more advanced model of live virtual reference service.

You should now be getting an inkling as to why so many librarians are excited about live virtual reference. It's a new way to bring human help to users at their desktops. With live virtual reference, users can receive human assistance whether they are sit-

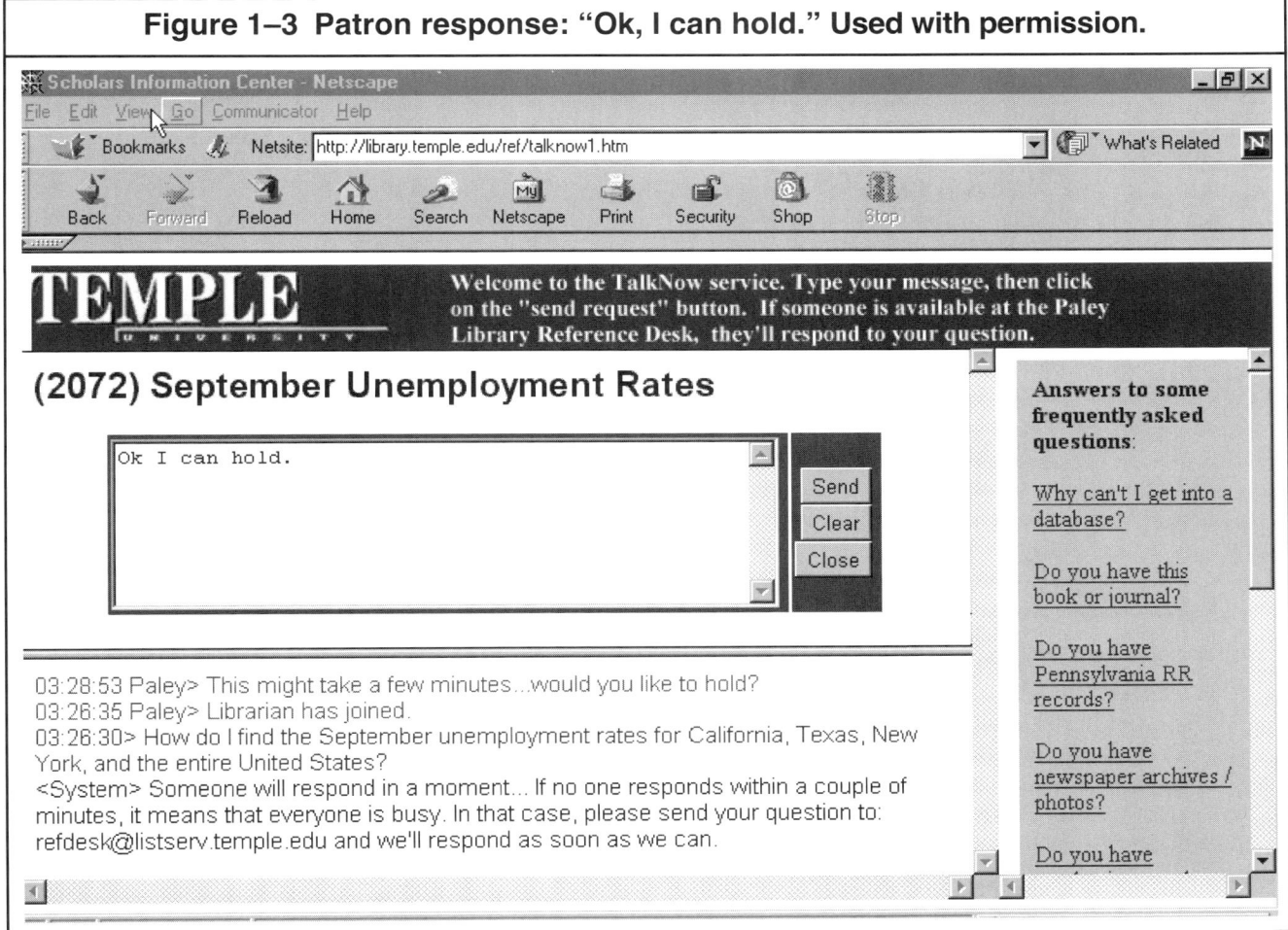

Figure 1–3 Patron response: "Ok, I can hold." Used with permission.

ting at a bank of workstations in the library, at their homes, in their offices, or at locations hundreds of miles away from the library. And just as patrons can receive help without entering the library, librarians can provide help to patrons without being at the library. In some versions of live virtual reference, librarians are not necessarily required to sit at the traditional physical reference desk. In fact, in most cases the physical reference desk just winds up getting in the way. Librarians can often provide better live virtual assistance from their offices in the library, from a different library branch or building, or from computers in their homes. Delivering service through the World Wide Web means that some users and librarians are no longer required to meet at a traditional reference desk to resolve information problems. What does this mean for the physical reference desk and other reference services?

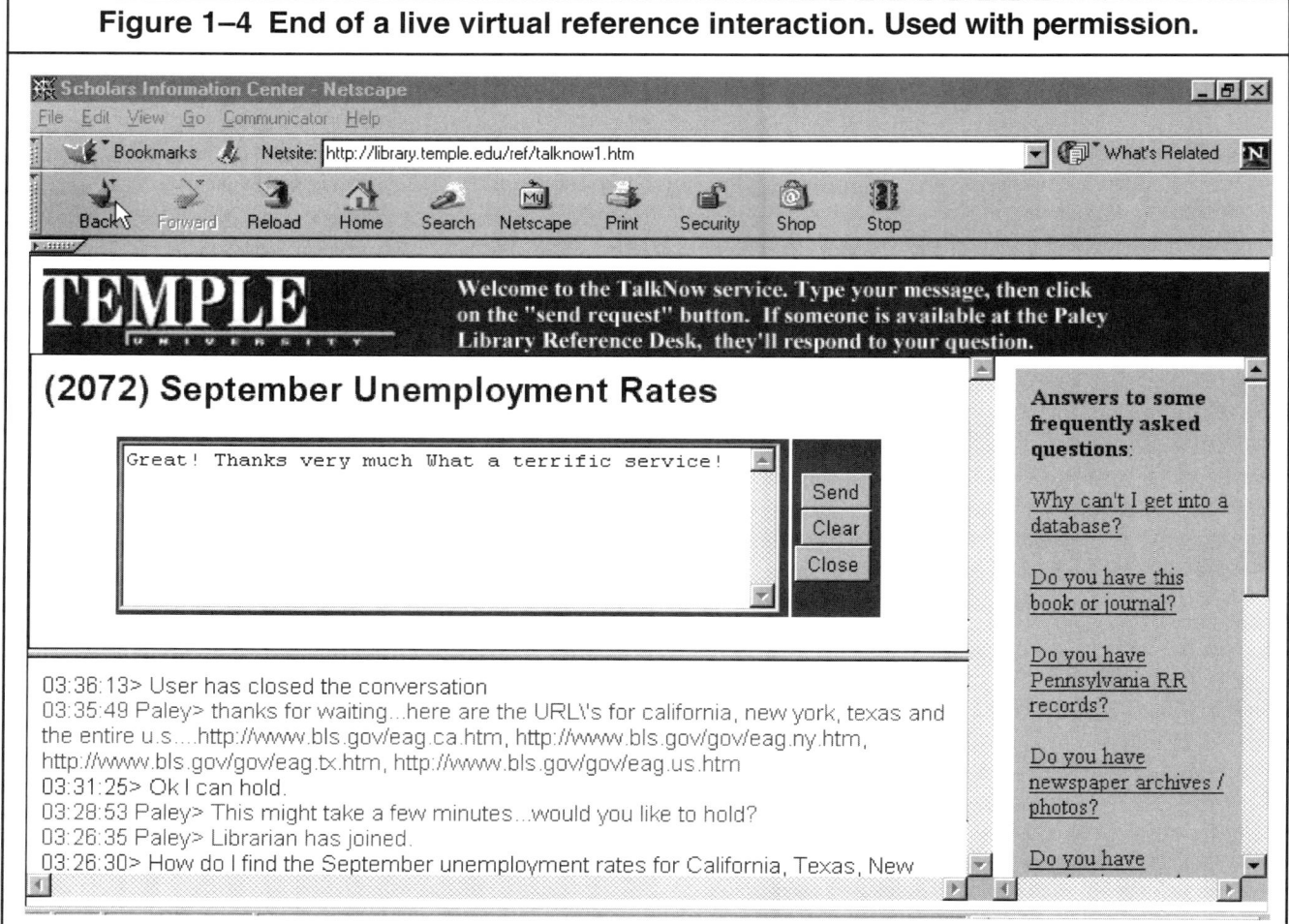

Figure 1–4 End of a live virtual reference interaction. Used with permission.

LIVE VIRTUAL REFERENCE COMPARED TO OTHER FORMS OF REFERENCE

Reference service now comes in many flavors. Face-to-face in-person desk reference. Telephone reference. E-mail virtual reference. Live virtual reference. We also have 24/7 services, Ask-A services, and collaborative services. Librarians who are unfamiliar with some of these newer services may have trouble, at least initially, keeping them all straight. Especially since some features can be combined with others, and since some librarians use phrases such as "virtual reference" or "digital reference" or "24/7" without being precise about what they are referring to. In this section we discuss some of the differences and similarities between live virtual reference and other important forms of reference.

FACE-TO-FACE IN-PERSON DESK REFERENCE

Live virtual reference is different from face-to-face in-person desk reference. Communication in live virtual reference takes place over a computer network; communication in face-to-face reference occurs, well, face-to-face. Since we are all pretty much familiar with face-to-face communication, we don't need much training in how to do it. That is, there is no technology to learn in the actual act of interacting with a patron face-to-face. Communication in live virtual reference is mediated by the computer, face-to-face communication is unmediated. That is not to say there are no subtleties in picking up the tone of voice, facial expressions, and body language of in-person patrons. For most people, these oral and visual clues that are absent in live virtual reference greatly facilitate in-person communication. Combined with the fact that we have been "practicing" face-to-face communication for most of our lives, face-to-face communication is definitely much easier (especially at first) than communicating by Internet text-messaging.

Face-to-face in-person reference also provides a level of personal service that is difficult if not impossible to match in virtual services. There simply is nothing like talking to someone face-to-face. Can we conclude from this that face-to-face in-person reference is more effective or works better than virtual reference? If a face-to-face reference desk exists in a library building, but no one is there to ask a question, is it effective? By making more and more library resources available through the Internet, librarians have made it easier and easier for patrons to access the library without having to physically come into the library. Since librarians generally seek to facilitate access to information, this is seen by most as a good thing. The corresponding virtual reference service also facilitates access to information and is also a good thing. A reference service that requires or depends on patrons visiting the library is not a complete service in a virtual environment. Virtual access to information is not going away. Trying to fight remote access is like fighting the ocean. Rather than fight it, live virtual reference goes with it and provides a virtual version of the personalized human-to-human service that occurs at the physical reference desk.

Does live virtual reference therefore entail the elimination of face-to-face service? Absolutely not. As long as library buildings continue to exist and patrons continue to enter them, libraries will need face-to-face reference desks where librarians can mediate between users and collections of information. But does this mean all reference interactions must occur face-to-face? Of course not! The hundreds of libraries that have successfully implemented live virtual reference services have shown that it is possible to provide valuable real-time reference help to library users who are using the virtual library. Live virtual reference and face-to-face in-person reference can and should peacefully coexist. Not only can they coexist, they can enhance and support each other. (However, for an example of a live virtual service without an in-person component, see the corporate call center model in Chapter 3.)

TELEPHONE REFERENCE

Although this may seem obvious, live virtual reference is not telephone reference. Some smart aleck in your library or consortium may object to the idea of live virtual reference on the grounds that if people want to talk to us in real-time they can just pick up the telephone. We actually encountered this very objection when we started our live service. Indeed, some librarians still voice this objection (Tyckoson, 1999). Although it's true that users can call the desk by telephone, if your users are on the Web, they may not be able to use the phone because their only line may be connected to their computer. In addition, you may want to provide real-time help to students who are in computer labs that don't have phones. Patrons in the remote nether regions of your library may not want to make the hike to your reference desk. Or maybe they just don't want to sacrifice their valuable seat at their workstation and have to pick up all their personal belongings. But everyone now has a cell phone you may say. Maybe so, but long URLs are very cumbersome to communicate over the phone, but easy to transmit over text-based chat, and even easier with page pushing or co-browsing. Live virtual reference is real-time like the telephone, but you don't need a telephone to use it, only a telephone or data line. It also has the added benefit that, unlike the user only listening to a librarian's advice over the phone, a live, virtual reference user can see the interaction on the computer screen.

E-MAIL VIRTUAL REFERENCE

Live virtual reference is related to but different from e-mail virtual reference. E-mail virtual reference, which is often called digital reference, does take place over the Internet, but not in real-time. In e-mail virtual reference, a patron may submit a question at almost any time of the day or night, but they will have to wait until a librarian retrieves the question and answers it to get a response. Response times vary, but most libraries post policies of answering e-mail reference questions within 24 hours. For some questions and some patrons, this can be very effective. A patron may not need an immediate answer to a reference question, and they may be willing to wait a day or so for a complete, accurate answer. Many may not mind the asymmetry between the time when the question is submitted and the time when the question is answered. Reference librarians, for their part, can take their time and not feel pressured to provide an answer at the very moment that the question is posed to them. Some librarians are staunch supporters of e-mail reference to the point that they claim it is superior to live virtual reference. We feel that the relationship is more one of symbiosis. Live virtual reference and e-mail reference support each other. Many questions *can* be answered in realtime, which is a faster way to serve patrons. Some, however, may require more time. If these questions are submitted through a live service, you can offer to the patron: "can I get back to you by e-mail?" Thus you give the patron the feeling that a live human being is handling their question, and that the question is being worked on. Live virtual reference and e-mail reference are two different ways of reaching the same goal, providing human help to library users. Live virtual reference takes place in real-time, e-mail reference does not. Live virtual reference and e-mail virtual reference are two different incarnations of virtual reference, but they are not the same thing. If someone uses the phrase "virtual reference," ask them if they are referring to live virtual reference or e-mail virtual reference.

24/7 REFERENCE

Live virtual reference is not synonymous with 24/7 reference. The idea of providing human help 24 hours a day, 7 days a week to researchers anywhere at anytime has been made somewhat more plausible and achievable by a reference service delivered through the Internet, since both users and librarians need not be in the same physical building. But live virtual reference is not equivalent to 24/7, it is not synonymous with 24/7, it does not require 24/7 operation. You can operate a live virtual reference service only during the hours your physical desk is open, you can operate it only during weekday evenings, or you can operate it only during the afternoons. With the exception of the CLEVNET, the Northern Illinois Alliance Library System, and North Carolina State University, the vast majority of libraries offering live virtual reference are not offering anything approaching live 24/7 service. Of the libraries that are offering 24/7, most report very low usage statistics for the overnight hours, and many outsource the answering of these questions to off-site librarians. Unfortunately, some librarians occasionally slip nonchalantly between live virtual reference and 24/7 reference as if they are the same thing. Some librarians may even claim that e-mail virtual reference is 24/7, which in a way it is, but that's really cheating. In e-mail virtual reference, it's true a patron may submit a question at 2:00 a.m., but the librarian may not get around to answering it until the next day. That's not true 24/7. In addition, a live virtual reference software product is called "24/7," which will undoubtedly continue to confuse matters. People continue to conflate 24/7 and live virtual reference. But 24/7 hours are certainly not mandatory, not necessary, and not required. Not even as a distant, future goal.

COLLABORATIVE REFERENCE

Live virtual reference is not necessarily collaborative reference. Collaborative reference is two or more libraries deciding to work together and share resources (staff, hardware, software) to offer reference services to users at participating institutions. Again, although a reference service delivered through the Internet may make collaboration between librarians at different institutions easier, it is not required. You can collaborate with libraries in your region, state, or even throughout the world. But you don't have to. Delivering reference through the Internet makes many innovative and exciting reference services possible. But the core of live virtual reference service is real-time human help delivered through the Internet.

ASK-A REFERENCE

Live virtual reference should not to be confused with an Ask-A service, as in AskERIC, Ask Dr. Math, Ask A Scientist, or Ask A Vulcanologist. In their excellent book, *The AskA Starter Kit*, Lankes and Kasowitz defined digital reference services as services that connect library users with individuals who have specialized subject knowledge or expertise (Lankes and Kasowitz 1998). This definition of digital reference is slightly different from the one we advance here. Although AskERIC has a real-time component, at this time most Ask-A services are not in real-time. Also, they are mostly aimed at the K–12 community. Again, although a live virtual reference could connect users with experts to answer their questions immediately, this is by no means required. Our conception concentrates on a more traditional notion of reference in which librarians mediate between users and a collection of information, instead of a service that connects users directly with experts.

REMOTE PATRON REFERENCE

We'd like to emphasize that live virtual reference is not necessarily for "remote" patrons only. Since many patrons access library resources from a number of locations, live virtual reference does not have to be a service for users who are at an extreme distance, although that is definitely one of its main attractions. Live virtual reference is about increasing the number of service options for users. Wherever they are. If this means some users feel more comfortable "chatting" with a reference librarian over the Internet than walking up to the physical desk, even when they are in the library, why force them to do what they don't want to do? During a 1999 keynote address at the Information Online Conference in Sydney, Anne Lipow coined a phrase and a philosophy that has become something of a rallying point among live virtual reference librarians: "it is we who are remote from our users.... We need to change how we do business in such a way as to get us back together" (Lipow, 1999). This phrase may have resonated so deeply with so many because it is both literal and metaphorical: librarians and potential library users are not only physically remote from each other, but mentally separated as well. The very idea of going to the library for information is foreign to many people. We just aren't on their radar screens. Old-school librarians who insist that patrons visit the physical reference desk ("why don't they just come to the desk!") wish for what once was but is no longer. The rules have changed. We need to reach our users where they are, or else we may not have any users left to reach.

WHAT IS LIVE VIRTUAL REFERENCE CALLED?

The number of terms used to describe varying types of virtual reference services can be bewildering. You may encounter virtual reference, digital reference, chat reference, electronic reference, Web-based reference, Ask-A-Librarian, online reference, interactive reference, live reference, live online reference, live interactive reference, online interactive reference, instant messaging, text messaging, call messaging, 24/7 reference, and reference in a MOO. And that's just in libraries. In the world of e-commerce, companies use expressions such as live assistance, live interaction, Web call center, live customer support, customer contact management and customer relationship management (CRM). The software for digital reference is variously described as chat software, instant messaging, Web contact center software, call center management software, live interactive communications utilities, and interactive customer assistance systems. Perhaps all this terminology will be simplified soon and we will all begin to use standardized terms. But don't count on it. For now, we need to keep all these terms straight and agree on some basic assumptions.

We have chosen the phrase *live virtual reference* for the following reasons. The phrases "digital reference," "virtual reference," or "electronic reference" are all too broad—they include a whole suite of services, including e-mail reference, which is not in real-time. "Chat reference" at least captures the real-time aspect, but it is really too narrow, since with some software you can go beyond chat with features such as page pushing, co-browsing, application sharing, and file transfer. "Interactive reference" is broader than "chat reference" but again it is too broad. After all, isn't all reference, including face-to-face in-person reference interactive? "Live reference," is a useful shorthand, but unfortunately it has the same problem. Even the most corpse-like reference librarians who seem to be frozen in a perpetual pointing stance are still "live" last time we checked. Some of the earliest real-time experiments were MOOs (Multiuser Object Oriented environments). MOOs, however, are really more descriptive of a chat "room" than a one-to-one environment (Henderson, 1994). Instant messaging is too closely tied to America Online's product, Instant Messenger. So we have settled on *live virtual reference*.

In *live virtual reference*, "live" corresponds to the notion of real-time service, which we believe is a crucial distinguishing feature. "Live" communicates the idea that your formerly dead Web page has now come "alive" with human help. "Virtual" expresses the idea that the service is an electronic attempt to simulate physical reference through the Internet. The word "reference" expresses the idea of human mediation and is associated with the traditional service of the physical reference desk with which librarians are familiar. *Live virtual reference*, therefore, is the way we describe what we are talking about in this book. We could just as easily have chosen the phrases real-time reference or live online reference, or live digital reference, but we will use the phrase *live virtual reference* as much as possible for clarity's sake. We may occasionally refer to it as live reference or chat reference or real-time reference, which are convenient shorthand terms. We're not militant about what it's called, but we do want to make sure we're all on the same page and using the same terms to describe the same thing.

One more point. Although we use *live virtual reference* for the purposes of this book, we wouldn't expect users to understand this phrase as the name of a service. What you decide to name your service for your users is a different matter. One of the most popular names for virtual reference services on the user side is "Ask A Librarian." This communicates clearly what the service is about for the user. Also popular are Ask Us! or Ask Us Live! If you give your service what you think is a cute or hip name, just make sure your users know what it is you are talking about.

SUMMARY

Live virtual reference *is* new, but it's not *that* new. Although it sounds more exciting to call live virtual reference a revolution, it's really more of an evolution that is rooted in the traditional values of reference service: one-on-one personal help for library users. There are many differences between using the Internet to help patrons and sitting at a physical desk in a physical library, which we will discuss in future chapters. These differences may be upsetting to some and may feel like large scale change. But if you always remember that live virtual reference is really grounded in traditional reference services, making the transition to this new form of reference will be much easier. We have a duty to our virtual patrons to add virtual reference to the virtual library. By not losing touch with our traditional values, virtual patrons will receive answers to their virtual queries that are as accurate, complete, timely, and personalized as any they would receive at a physical desk. Live virtual reference brings one of the most successful and popular library services—reference—into the digital age.

REFERENCES

Coffman, Steve, and Susan McGlamery. 2000. "The Librarian and Mr. Jeeves." *American Libraries* (May): 66–69.

Gorman, Michael. 2001. "Values for Human-to-Human Reference." *Library Trends* 50, no. 2 (Fall): 168–182.

Green, Samuel S. 1876. "Personal Relations Between Librarians and Readers." *American Library Journal* 1 (2–3): 74–81.

Henderson, Tona. 1994. "MOOving Towards a Virtual Reference Service." *The Reference Librarian* 41/42: 173–184.

Lankes, R. David, and Abby S. Kasowitz. 1998. *The AskA Starter Kit: How to Build and Maintain Digital Reference Services*. Syracuse, N.Y.: ERIC Clearinghouse on Information and Technology.

Lipow, Anne G. 1999. Serving the remote user: reference service in the digital environment. Paper presented at the Ninth Australasian Information Online and On Disc Conference and Exhibition, 19–21 January, at Sydney Convention and Exhibition Centre, Sydney Australia. Available online at www.csu.edu.au/special/online99/proceedings99/200.htm [2002, April 29].

Tyckoson, David A. 1999. "What's Right with Reference." *American Libraries* 5 (May, 30): 57–61.

Whitson, William L. 1995. "Differentiated Service: A New Reference Model." *The Journal of Academic Librarianship* (March): 103–110.

2 OFFERING LIVE VIRTUAL REFERENCE

Why offer live virtual reference? Live virtual reference is becoming a more and more accepted part of reference services because of its effectiveness in reaching virtual patrons. It also has its detractors. Some of these detractors may be your own skeptical colleagues. If you need some ammunition to convince doubters, naysayers, and unbelievers, here are ten compelling reasons to offer live virtual reference. Use them on yourself, your colleagues, your co-workers, your director, your potential collaborators, or anyone else you need to convince about the desirability of live virtual reference. We'll also present some obstacles and suggest how they might be overcome.

TEN REASONS TO OFFER LIVE VIRTUAL REFERENCE

SERVE USERS WHERE THEY ARE SEARCHING

There's no denying that large numbers of people use the Internet everyday, and that a breathtaking amount of information is easily accessible there. Before the Internet, information seekers had almost no choice but to begin their searches at physical libraries. Now, simple searches initiated at search engines often yield astounding results. The amount of information that is available on the Web, the convenience of searching from home, the willingness of many to accept information that is good enough for their purposes, the hype about how "everything is on the Internet," all contribute to a movement away from the physical library as a place to find information. Patrons who once visited the library can have their information needs fulfilled by the World Wide Web.

Statistics and anecdotal evidence indicate that reference questions in almost all libraries have declined by between 6 percent and 15 percent the past few years (Coffman and McGlamery 2000). Exactly why this has happened and whether there will continue to be a long-term downward trend is unclear. Perhaps the day that the Internet puts reference librarians out of a job may never come. But even reasonable librarians who aren't normally prone to fear and paranoia may worry that one day, no reference questions will amount to no reference librarians. These librarians should be asking themselves, "questions are going down, what can we do to better serve our users?"

Live virtual reference is one answer. It's something positive and proactive to do instead of sitting passively at the physical reference desk. Although it's true that some patrons use the Internet with ease and success, many also encounter a great deal of frustration when their searches aren't successful. Even though everything is supposed to be on the Internet, often it isn't, or it isn't easy to find for those who don't know where to look. Shouldn't these confused searchers have a real live person to turn to for help, just as they do in the physical library?

Librarians need to be where patrons are to guide them in their search. We provide access to our print collections through Web-based catalogs, we make periodical articles available through aggregated Web databases, we digitize parts of our collections. Most of us already provide virtual access to reference librarians through e-mail. Live virtual reference is the next logical step. It allows us to continue to serve users who are now on the Web who would have previously been in the library, or those who never have visited the library. If there's one thing that the advent of the Internet means for reference librarians, it's that it's unwise to wait passively for users to show up at the physical reference desk. Let's go where they are—the Internet.

KEEP UP WITH RISING EXPECTATIONS

Staying competitive means keeping up with continually rising expectations. Many companies involved in e-commerce see the value of live interactivity to their bottom line and have added it to their Web sites. If our users can chat in real-time to customer service representatives at Lands' End, 1-800-Flowers, and Mailboxes Etc., why shouldn't they expect the same level of service at their library? If a patron can't get an answer to their question now, they will leave the library site and look elsewhere. Instead of complaining about our patrons' willingness to accept "low quality" information sources, we need to focus on meeting their expectations of immediacy and convenience. Live virtual reference enables libraries to keep pace with the rest of the world in providing access to human help on the World Wide Web.

ANSWER QUESTIONS WITH FASTER RESPONSE TIME

E-mail virtual reference is an established and valuable piece of virtual reference service. But it may not be enough. The concept and procedure can definitely be improved. If the number of questions you receive through your e-mail service has been disappointing, perhaps you need to take e-mail reference up a notch by providing live, real-time service. Some patrons may not mind waiting for a response to their e-mail, but other patrons are better served by a quick answer to a quick question. They don't want to wait hours for an e-mail answer. In the first six week period that we had our real-time service up at Temple University, we received 86 questions in real-time compared with 54 questions through our established e-mail reference service. Throughout the first three years of real-time operation, real-time questions consistently outnumbered e-mail questions. Think about it. If you ask me a question, would you rather I answer you right now, or would you be satisfied with an e-mail tomorrow? If given the choice, most people prefer real-time answers to their questions over e-mail answers that require a longer wait when this is possible.

CONDUCT VIRTUAL REFERENCE INTERVIEWS

Although e-mail reference works well for many queries, it's not a very efficient way to conduct that crucial part of the reference transaction, the reference interview. Live virtual reference allows you to go back and forth with a patron as you would at the physical reference desk, but are unable to do in e-mail reference. This saves you and the user time as you get down to what information the person is really looking for. Live virtual reference adds more interactivity to your Web site by allowing you to conduct reference interviews in real-time.

SHOW INSTEAD OF TELL

Live virtual reference has more features than e-mail virtual reference. Instead of describing the path to a Web page or explaining a search strategy in words, you can show your users by pushing Web pages and escorting users with co-browsing. This is particularly true with the more sophisticated live virtual reference software programs. They allow you to sync up with your patron's browser and escort them to Web sites. For many patrons, showing can be more effective than telling. These advanced features are also very attractive to many librarians, and a demonstration often sells them on why they need to do live virtual reference instead of e-mail virtual reference.

SERVE DISTANCE LEARNERS

The trend toward live virtual reference dovetails with the trend in education toward distance learning. More and more students of varying ages are taking entire classes online without visiting physical classrooms or physical libraries. These people may be miles away from their institutions' library, yet they still have research needs. Their research needs include access to library services as well as text-based resources. These people deserve equal access. You can no longer fall back on the excuse of giving priority to in-person patrons. Live virtual reference is a way to provide equal service to distance learners.

CONNECT WITH THE NEW GENERATION

It is well known that real-time communication, chat, is enormously popular with children, teenagers, and college students. You might even call it an obsession. This is certainly part of their everyday lives. What library can afford to pass up the chance to associate itself with something so popular with these age groups? By offering a service on their terms, you can make an instant connection to the way they do things. Anytime a library has an opportunity to present itself as not old and stodgy, we need to take advantage of it. Libraries such as the Morris County Library in New Jersey, the CLEVNET consortium in Ohio, the King County Library in Seattle, and many others, have initiated chat reference experiments and pilot projects with the specific intention of reaching young adults for homework help. Not only will you be providing a convenient service, you'll be connecting with future life-long library users.

EMPOWER USERS WITH DIFFERING ABILITIES

Libraries are required by the Americans with Disabilities Act to provide reasonable accommodations for people with differing abilities. This of course means many things, from providing wheelchair ramps to offering a text version of your graphic intensive Web page. Live virtual reference is yet another way to reach out to users who, for whatever reason, may be unable or uncomfortable approaching the physical reference desk. A person with a physical disability may have trouble getting to your reference desk. A person with a hearing impairment may not be able to use the telephone. Live virtual reference gives these users yet another option in receiving reference service.

CREATE EXCITEMENT AND LEARN CUTTING-EDGE SKILLS

Live virtual reference is on the cutting edge of reference services. Being on the cutting edge can be risky, but it also creates excitement. Grantmakers are more likely to get excited about and support new initiatives than established ones. Administrators like to present their institution as being on the cutting edge. Library staff

10 Reasons to Offer Live Virtual Reference
1. Serve users where they are searching
2. Keep up with rising expectations
3. Answer questions with faster response time
4. Conduct virtual reference interviews
5. Show instead of tell
6. Serve distance learners
7. Connect with the new generation
8. Empower users with differing abilities
9. Create excitement and learn new skills by being on the cutting edge
10. Pursue marketing and relationship building

can be jolted out of a rut by doing something new. One librarian told us that live reference helped him to get energized about doing reference again. Librarians get to learn new skills and help new patrons in a new way. And patrons are more likely to smile in delight when they chat with a librarian instead of using the telephone. There's something neat about seeing a Web page come to life with the words of a real person. The novelty of live virtual reference communicates to your patrons, staff, and administrators that your library is a leader in the areas of technology and service to your key stakeholders.

PURSUE MARKETING AND RELATIONSHIP BUILDING

Hype and distortion about the power of technology engender misunderstandings about the nature of information and the services that libraries offer. By giving your patrons the opportunity to speak to a librarian in real-time through the Internet, you give your library an opportunity to market and promote itself. Every successful live virtual reference transaction communicates the idea that librarians are experts at finding information, and that turning to a real live librarian can be faster and better than turning to an Internet search engine. Live virtual reference creates chances for the library to make new friends and to build relationships with patrons who will keep coming back. Our old mindset may have been that we needed to limit demand for personal service else we be overwhelmed with users. Our new mindset should be that we need to create demand by educating users about the ease, quality, and authority of library information services and sources.

TEN OBSTACLES TO OVERCOME WHEN OFFERING LIVE VIRTUAL REFERENCE

COPING WITH ADDITIONAL WORKLOAD

Workload is surely one of the biggest if not the biggest obstacle to setting up a live virtual reference service. Although it's true that traditional desk questions are decreasing, traditional reference desks still receive much more traffic than virtual reference desks. This means that it is seldom possible to simply transfer the staffing from a physical desk to a virtual desk. The physical desk will have to be maintained. The dilemma of staffing a live virtual reference desk is how do you staff a new service point, while maintaining the old one? Putting it another way, how can your librarians be in two places at once? Is it fair to ask your librarians to do more work with no increase in staff? Will your unionized librarians revolt? Will your faculty librarians stand for it?

Complicating the situation, the work involved in setting up a live reference service is more than just answering the questions, it's planning, writing policies, training staff, monitoring and evaluating answer quality, dealing with software and hardware problems, and promoting the service with publicity. It's a total package. Who will do this work and where will the time come from? Is the number of questions you are answering and the number of people you are serving worth all the work and time you are putting into it?

Libraries have tried a variety of techniques to deal with these problems, from juggling live questions with in-person questions at the physical desk, to asking for volunteers, to collaborating with other libraries, and hiring new staff. Solving staffing challenges is the most important obstacle to overcome in offering real-time reference. We'll devote a full chapter to it in Chapter 6.

GENERATING INITIAL AND CONTINUED SUPPORT

Live virtual reference is often introduced into libraries by a few enthusiastic individuals. In order for live virtual reference to succeed, enthusiasm must be spread and consensus must be built among two key constituencies: the librarians who are going to be actually answering the questions, and the library administration. If the reference librarians are uncomfortable with the technology, resistant to learning, critical of the staffing arrangement, or afraid of change, your project will have problems. Some libraries have attempted to get over this obstacle by asking for volunteers to staff the new service. Besides the front-line librarians, you must have support from your library administration. If the library administration does not support live virtual reference, getting the necessary resources for the project will be a constant uphill battle.

FINDING QUALIFIED TECHNICAL PERSONNEL

You will need technical personnel to install software, maintain equipment, and troubleshoot problems. Technical problems will come up. The software that is supposed to work right out of the box will have glitches. The databases that you were supposed to be able to share with patrons will not work correctly because of a firewall. Patrons with frame-busting browsers may wreck your plans to push Web pages. Servers will go down. The vendor's vaunted customer service will not be able to help you. Live virtual reference service is not a self-cleaning oven. Things will break and someone will have to fix them.

CONTROLLING COSTS AND GETTING FUNDING

Another concern is cost. Getting started with one of the more sophisticated software packages could run up to $15,000 for the first year, and that's just for one seat (a seat is one librarian who is logged in) at a time. You'll pay more for each additional seat. If you want to run the software on your own server and avoid the yearly fee you will pay considerably more. Running the program on your own server is desirable because you get to maintain some control and it will also mean faster communication between you and your patrons. The drawback is you have to have the systems staff to administer the server. There are less expensive software packages, but these programs have other drawbacks. Less expensive software has less fully developed features and less customer support. Companies that offer less expensive software are less established and may not be around for more than a few years. Then you'll have to select software again. There are even free software packages, but it is often said that free software is as free as a free kitten. You will have to spend much time nurturing and feeding, installing and configuring these programs. Ways around the high cost of software include teaming together with other libraries in a consortium, and obtaining external grant funding.

RE-ENVISIONING YOUR LIBRARY AS A VIRTUAL PLACE

Perhaps you don't want to encourage your patrons to ask questions through the Internet. You have just built a beautiful new library building and you want to encourage people to come to it. You have also spent a lot of money on reference books through the years and you want people to use them too. By opening a virtual service point you risk reducing the physical presence of your library. If your catalog is online, your databases are online, and your reference librarians are online, what is the physical library for? A counterargument to this claim is that virtual reference actually results in more people visiting the library. Many of your patrons may not even be aware that they have a library. After using virtual library services, patrons become more familiar with all library services, including the physical library.

DISPELLING FEAR OF THE UNKNOWN

Cold fear. Visceral and instinctive, irrational and deep-rooted, fear can be a stumbling block on your road to live virtual reference. We have been arguing that live virtual reference is firmly rooted in the values of traditional desk reference. Still, live virtual reference has enough destabilizing elements—reference without a desk, new modes of communicating, recorded transcripts of interactions—to scare the bejesus out of some people. For some librarians, the physical reference desk is so much a part of their notion of what it means to be a reference librarian that talk of a new way of delivering reference can cause all sorts of fears to come bubbling up to the surface. Fear of doing something new and changing the way things have always been can be significant. It's often much easier to cling to the old, familiar way of doing things instead of leaping into the unknown. This can be manifested in naysaying—"this will not work!"; nitpicking—"this software stinks!"; groundless worrying—"what if we get bombarded with hundreds (thousands!) of questions? *Per hour!* From people all over the world!"

Fortunately, once they get over the initial fear factor, most librarians are very good at adapting to change and applying new technologies to library services. Look at the World Wide Web. Until the mid 1990s, most people hadn't even heard of the World Wide Web. Now, it's hard to imagine not using the Web. It's become thoroughly integrated into all library work. Librarians have become comfortable with it. Ok, so a few retired, but current practitioners have adapted quite impressively.

As far as large increases in questions, most libraries have not been overrun. The potential for an increase in traffic is real, but not likely, especially in the early stages of the service. One way to head off this fear is to have a clear policy that limits users to your community instead of opening the service up to the entire Internet.

RECOGNIZING LIMITATIONS TO TEXT-BASED CHAT

Communicating by text-based chat over the Internet has its problems. It's not the same as communicating face-to-face or by phone. It can take longer to explain relatively simple things. If a miscommunication does occur, it can be even more difficult to clear up by chat. You may have to resort to calling the person. Honestly, text-based chat cannot do everything. Some in the live reference community think that Voice Over Internet Protocol (VoIP), will solve this problem. But VoIP has its own problems. Although it seems to be perpetually "just around the corner" VoIP is not yet widespread. The quality of voice transmission is still too rudimentary for reference. Even if VoIP becomes widespread, there's still some reason to continue service by text-based chat. There is something very quick and simple about a text-based interchange. Some socio-phobic patrons and librarians may actually prefer to handle some questions by chat instead of voice. The more communication options we can provide, the better. Just because text-based chat can't do everything in-person communication can do, that's not a good enough reason not to do live virtual reference.

WORKING WITH CRANKY LIBRARY FACULTY

If you work in an academic library in which librarians have faculty status, the tenure process may work against introducing a live virtual reference service. The librarians who don't yet have tenure will ask, how is this going to help me get tenure? If it doesn't, or worse, if it takes time away from activities such as writing that will help them get tenure, they won't want to do it. The librarians who already have tenure, don't really have to do anything they don't want to do, so if they see the new service as new work that they don't have time for, they can obstruct the project. One way to get around this problem is to convince the tenure track librarians that a new service opens up all sorts of publication opportunities. If the tenured librarians see this as helping their junior colleagues get tenure, they may be willing to do it.

TROUBLE-SHOOTING SUNDRY TECHNICAL HEADACHES

Since live virtual reference involves technology, all sorts of technical meltdowns could quickly become part of your life. The software you choose could mess up your hardware or interfere with your other programs. You could have downloading and installing issues about installing software on machines in the library, about patrons installing software on their machines, and librarians installing software on the machines in their offices or their machines at home. Speaking of home, how fast are your librarians' connections at home? How about your patrons? Getting co-browsing software to work with proxy databases is also a frequently heard problem. Some of these issues can be solved or sidestepped with good planning, but live virtual reference, like

> **10 Obstacles to Overcome When Offering Live Virtual Reference**
>
> 1. Coping with additional workload
> 2. Generating initial and continued support
> 3. Finding qualified technical personnel
> 4. Controlling costs and getting funding
> 5. Re-envisioning the library as a virtual place
> 6. Dispelling fear of the unknown
> 7. Recognizing limitations to text-based chat
> 8. Working with cranky library faculty
> 9. Trouble-shooting sundry technical headaches
> 10. Understanding copyright and renegotiating licenses

the Internet, is still in the relatively early stages. It's likely that when these problems are solved, others will arise.

UNDERSTANDING COPYRIGHT AND RENEGOTIATING LICENSES

Does copyright law and your current database licenses permit you to push pages of a proprietary database to your patrons? What about to patrons who don't attend your institution or are not in your state? What about escorting them to a database and leaving them there? Will you ever be able to tell for sure who is really in your state or not? Guess what: no one really knows the answers to these questions. Approaches are still evolving. For the time being, the simplest solution is to play it safe and follow your licensing agreements. In the future, start thinking about how to renegotiate licenses to accommodate live virtual reference.

SUMMARY

Of all the reasons to offer live virtual reference, one of the most important is that our users are on the Internet, so we must be too. Virtual reference has an inevitability to it—the future seems to be on its side. If the future is going to come anyway, might as well start now. But there are other reasons to offer live virtual reference. Another is that librarians get to learn and apply new skills. Ultimately, a great hope for live virtual reference is that it reaches folks who otherwise would not have turned to the library for help.

> List your reasons for doing live virtual reference on the left and your obstacles to overcome on the right. Count the total for each side and circle your biggest reason and biggest obstacle.
>
> Reasons for   Obstacles to overcome
> _____   _____
> _____   _____
> _____   _____
> _____   _____
> _____   _____
> _____   _____
> _____   _____

No doubt there are obstacles to offering live virtual reference too. Dealing with extra workload is one everyone has to struggle with. Making the transition from a physical desk to a virtual desk is another. The physical desk has an inertia to it. The past is on its side, and some librarians are reluctant to let the past go, sometimes for good reason. A great fear of staying with the physical reference desk too long is that our desks will exist, but there will be no patrons at those desks to ask questions.

You may have your own reasons or your own obstacles to offering live virtual reference. You may have a very simple reason to do it: your director told you so! Whether or not the reasons to offer live virtual reference outnumber the obstacles will depend a lot on your particular situation. Whatever obstacles you face, rest assured they can be overcome, as evidenced by the more than 200 libraries that are now offering live virtual reference. As an exercise for clarifying your thinking, take a sheet of paper and draw a line down the middle, or use the worksheet included above. Write your reasons for on one side and obstacles to overcome on the other, then add them up. Circle your biggest reason for live virtual reference and your biggest obstacle. Keep these in mind when you read about the five models of live digital reference in the next chapter. The model that addresses your motivations and reduces your obstacles has the best chance for succeeding at your library.

REFERENCES

Coffman, Steve, and Susan McGlamery. 2000. "The Librarian and Mr. Jeeves." *American Libraries* (May): 66–69.

3 EXPLORING THE FIVE MODELS OF LIVE VIRTUAL REFERENCE

There are five models of live virtual reference that affect current library practice: the basic model, the homegrown model, the advanced model, the collaborative model, and the corporate call center model. To some extent, the models exist on a continuum of simple to complex, inexpensive to expensive, individual to cooperative across a variety of different areas such as planning and policy, software and staffing. The advanced and collaborative models are becoming more and more popular because the software permits librarians to send Web pages to patrons and in the case of the collaborative model libraries can share costs and distribute staffing. Although the advanced and collaborative models get a lot of attention, they aren't the only options and may not be best for every situation. This section aims to give you an overview of the different philosophies and practices behind each of the models. Choose one model, or mix and match from the different approaches to create a model that best fits your library.

BASIC MODEL—FREE OR LOW COST CHAT

The basic model is the simplest, no-nonsense setup for live virtual reference. Although simple, the model can be very effective. It can be useful for librarians who want to get something up quickly, who do not have a lot of time or money, or who want to experiment. In the basic model, live virtual reference software is free or almost free, so only a very modest budget or grant is required. The software is usually hosted on a remote server, so the only hardware required is the desktop computer that the librarian is currently using. Software maintenance is not the library's responsibility. The software features are minimal, consisting mainly of Web-based text chat, so that a long period of staff training is not required. In fact, training often occurs on the job, as questioned are answered. Reference librarians operate the service

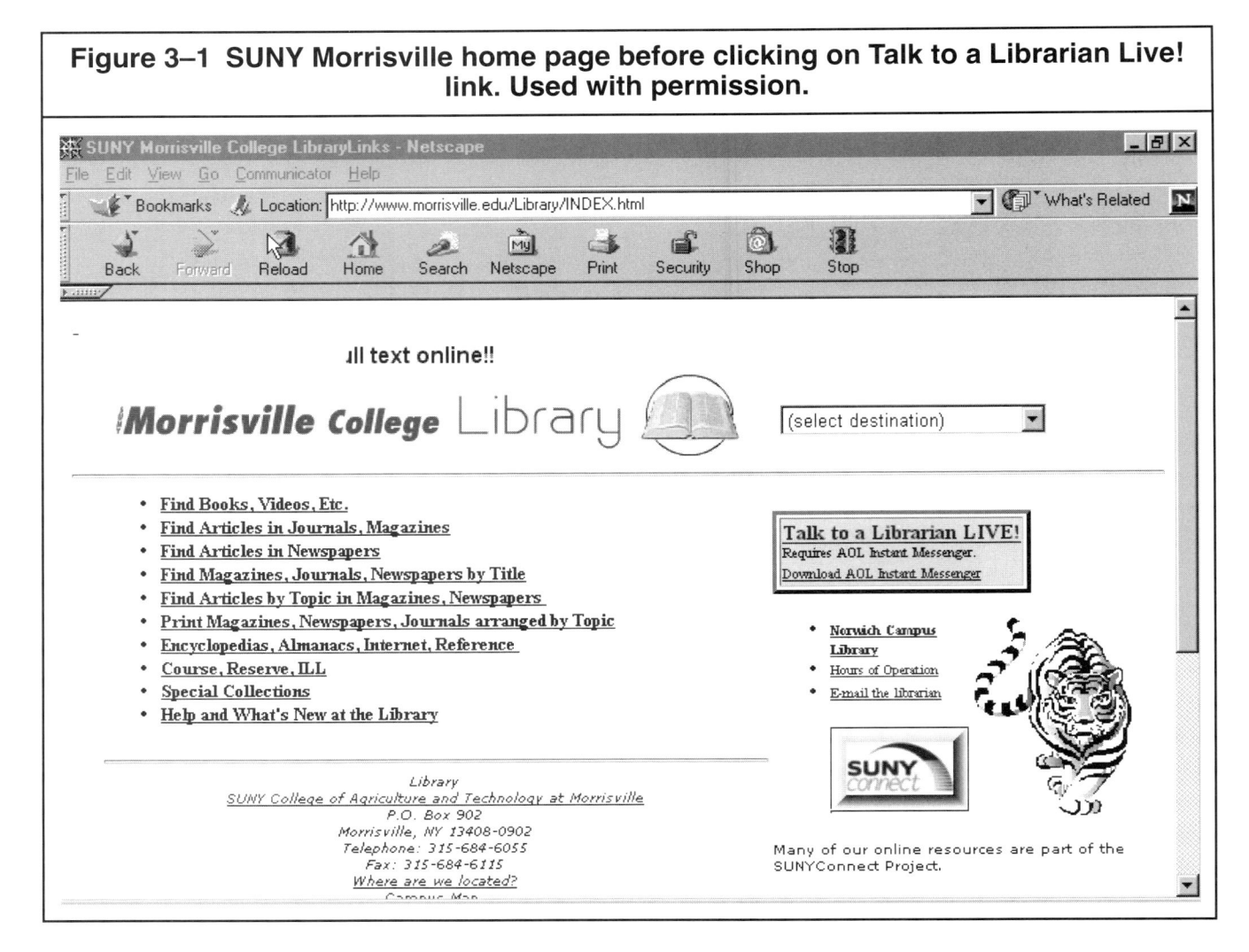

Figure 3–1 SUNY Morrisville home page before clicking on Talk to a Librarian Live! link. Used with permission.

while they are at the reference desk, so a second reference schedule is not required. The hours of the new service are the same as the physical reference desk. The whole issue of staffing is, in a way, sidestepped. Planning is also minimal; one or two enthusiastic librarians can implement the model, as long as they have the support of the librarians who will actually answer the questions.

An example of the basic model is the setup at the State University of New York at Morrisville. SUNY Morrisville was one of the first libraries to experiment with real-time reference in 1997 under the direction of systems librarian Bill Drew. Although the software used at Morrisville has changed over time, simplicity is still the guiding philosophy. The main point of the service is to provide real-time help to patrons by text-based chat. The service

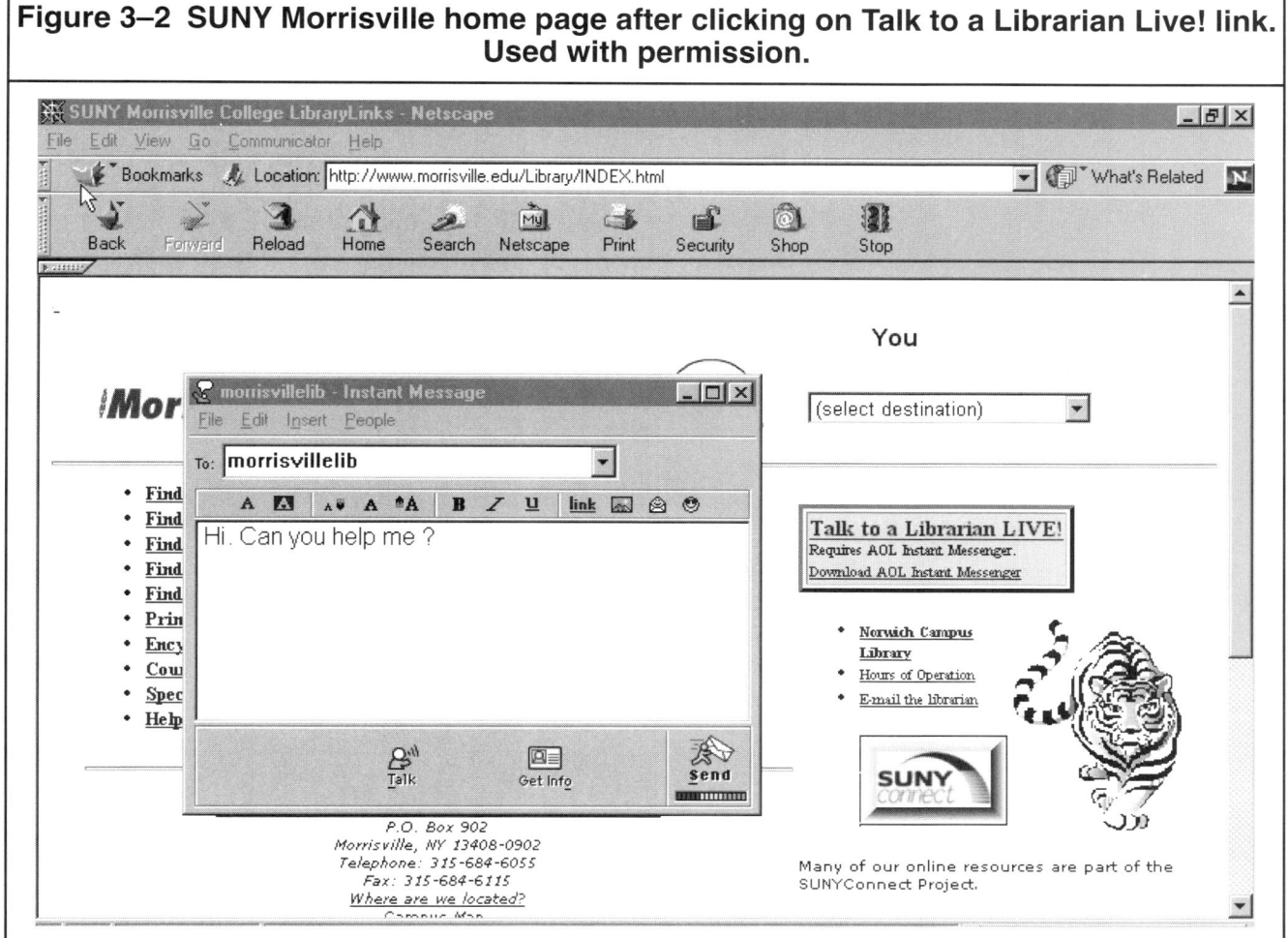

Figure 3–2 SUNY Morrisville home page after clicking on Talk to a Librarian Live! link. Used with permission.

at SUNY Morrisville is called Talk to a Librarian Live! The software is AOL Instant Messenger, which is downloadable for free and popular among college students. The patron is required to have the AOL Instant Messenger (IM) software installed on their computer and they must sign up for an account. Even though use of IM is widespread and many people do have accounts, the requirement to download software and activate an account can be a barrier to patrons asking questions. The main feature of the software is chatting in real time; fancy features such as page pushing or co-browsing are usually not available. It is possible, however, to send clickable html links through IM. The librarians at SUNY Morrisville serve real-time patrons while also serving patrons at the physical reference desk, simplifying staffing, but complicating their physical desk service. Figures 3–1 and 3–2 are

> **Basic Model Summary**
>
> - Simple but effective
> - Free or inexpensive software
> - Patron requirement to download software may be a barrier
> - No hardware required
> - Chatting or instant messaging main feature
> - No page pushing or co-browsing
> - Extensive staff training not required
> - Planning minimal
> - Software—AOL Instant Messenger, MSN Messenger, LivePerson, LiveHelper, LiveAssistance

simulated examples of what happens when a patron uses live virtual reference at SUNY Morrisville (all examples in this chapter are simulations and not samples of "real" patron questions). Figure 3-1 is SUNY Morrisville's Library home page before the patron clicks on the Talk to a Librarian Live! link. Figure 3-2 is after the patron clicks on the link.

As Figure 3-2 shows, when a user clicks on the Talk to a Librarian LIVE! link, an Instant Messenger window pops up with the screen name morrisvillelib in the "to" field. If the patron does not have AOL Instant Messenger, a link is provided for the person to download it. With AOL IM, the patron and the librarian can communicate by instant messages in real-time. Overall, the basic model is a simple, effective way to make use of widespread, free technology. Other software products for the basic model include MSN Messenger, LivePerson, LiveHelper, and Live Assistance. With the exception of MSN Messenger, these products are not free but they are inexpensive compared to other products.

HOMEGROWN MODEL—CREATE OR DOWNLOAD OPEN SOURCE SOFTWARE

The homegrown model is similar to the basic model, but slightly more complex. In the homegrown model, the library creates its own software product or uses freely available open source software instead of using commercial or commercially adapted software. This adds a level of complexity to the process since the library has to either write the program code for the software or download and install an existing program.

Open source software is software created by individual programmers and made available widely through free servers. People are free to download the software, use it, and modify it, as long as the software remains free to those who ask for it. Some examples of open source software in libraries are MyLibrary@NCState (my.lib.ncsu.edu), jake, which stands for jointly administered knowledge environment, and OpenBook, an open source library automation system developed by Technology Resource Foundation. (For a more complete list see www.oss4lib.org/projects/.) Open source creators often refer to open source as a "movement" and there is sort of a 60's spirit to all this free sharing and opposition to commercial products. For more on open source software in libraries, see www.oss4lib.org and the March 2002 issue of *Information Technology and Libraries*.

An advantage of the open source approach is that the library owns the software and does not have to worry about subscription costs. The library also avoids vendors who offer what start out as free products but then later on begin charging for them. Another advantage is that the library has more control over what features the software has and can tailor it to the library environment, instead of using a program that is more oriented for e-commerce. Although there is more labor involved in creating and setting up the software, the library does not have to go through the often time-consuming process of applying for and obtaining a grant to purchase software. A disadvantage is that open source software usually comes with little documentation and is seldom user-friendly.

Libraries that are using open source software include Temple University, Miami University (Ohio), and Southern Illinois University. At Temple, we were lucky enough to be able to enlist the help of two computer science students who wrote the software program for us. Unfortunately, we did not require them to write documentation, making it difficult for us to modify the software or make it available to others after the students went on to other projects. Other libraries have been more successful at creating software all libraries can share. Librarian Rob Casson at Miami University (Ohio) has created software called Rakim that is currently in use and available for download at styro.lib.muohio.edu/rakim/. Southern Illinois University is using homegrown open source software called Morris Messenger created by Keith VanCleave that is available at www.lib.siu.edu/chat/. Librarians Jody Condit Fagan and Michele Calloway describe the Morris

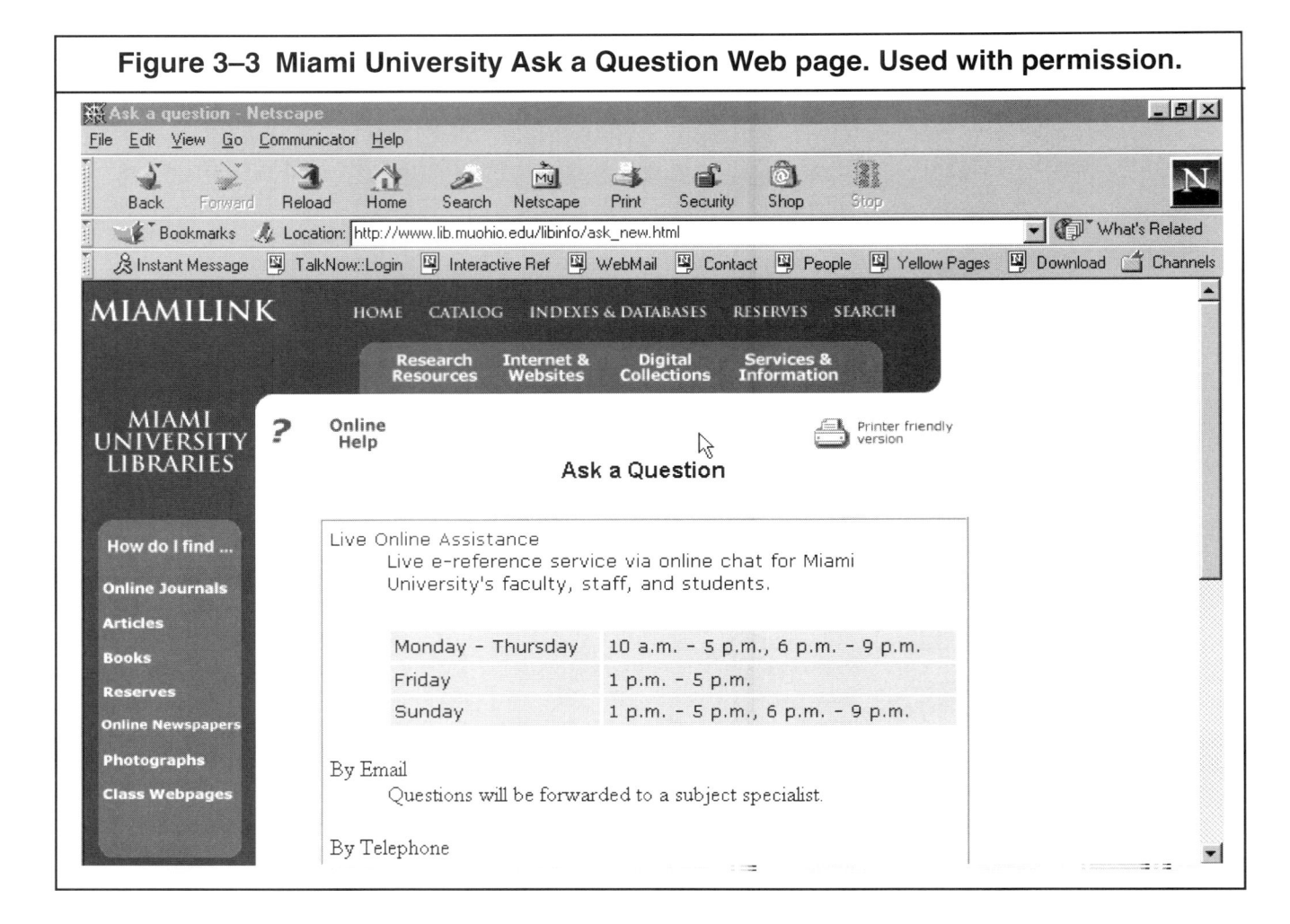

Figure 3–3 Miami University Ask a Question Web page. Used with permission.

Messenger software in detail in their article "Creating an Instant Messaging Reference System" (Fagan and Calloway, 2001).

You've already seen one example of a homegrown live virtual reference service in Chapter 1. Here's what the homegrown system created at Miami University (Ohio) looks like. In Figure 3–3, a patron is presented with a Web page of choices to contact the librarian: live chat, e-mail, and telephone.

After choosing live chat, a form appears (Figure 3–4) in which the patron is asked to fill in a screen name, an e-mail address, and other information.

Next, in Figure 3–5, the patron receives a text message from a librarian.

In Figure 3–6 the patron and the librarian interact in real-time through the Web form.

After the transaction is completed, the patron receives a transcript of the session, a nice feature (see Figure 3–7).

Figure 3–4 Miami University Live Online Assistance form. Used with permission.

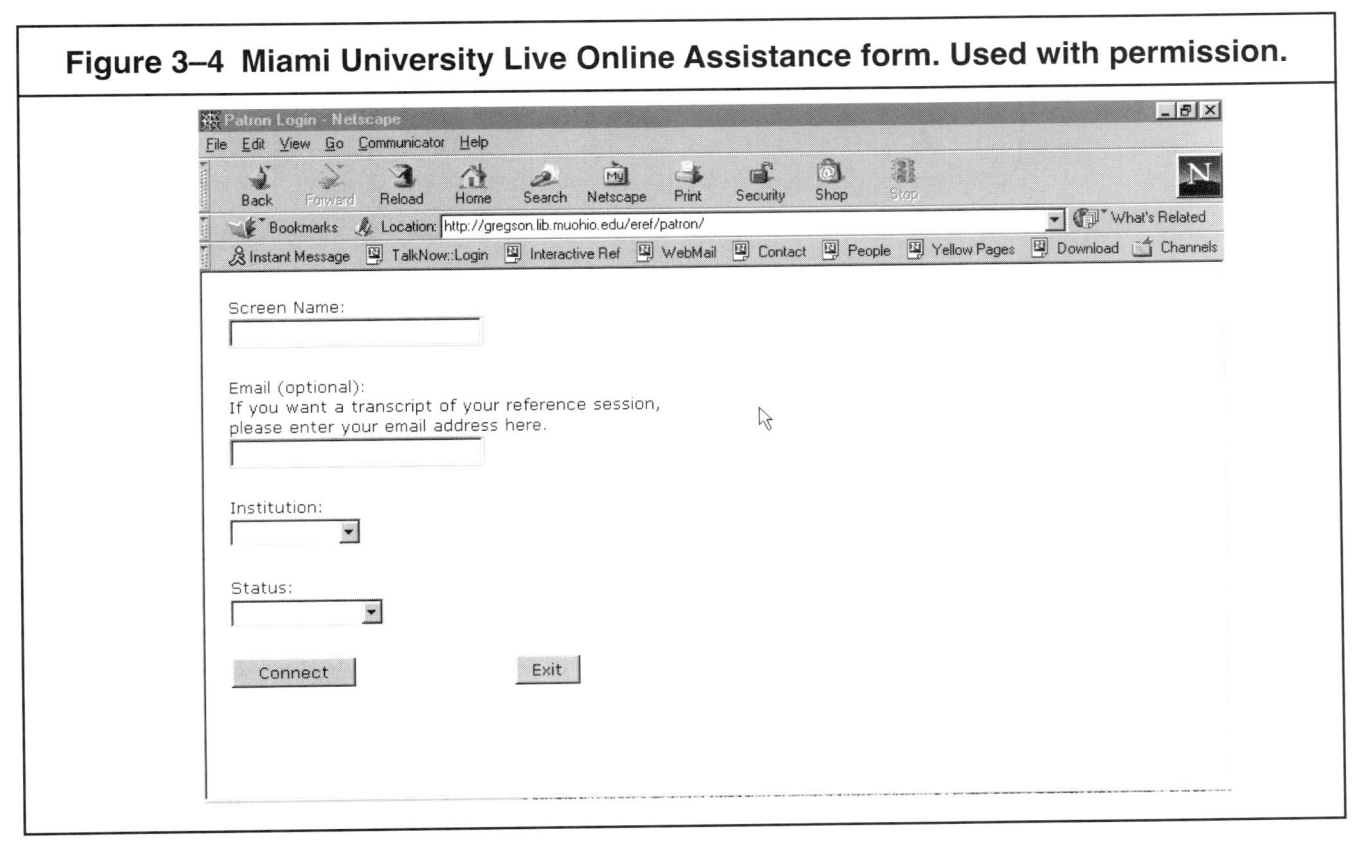

Figure 3–5 Miami University text message from a librarian. Used with permission.

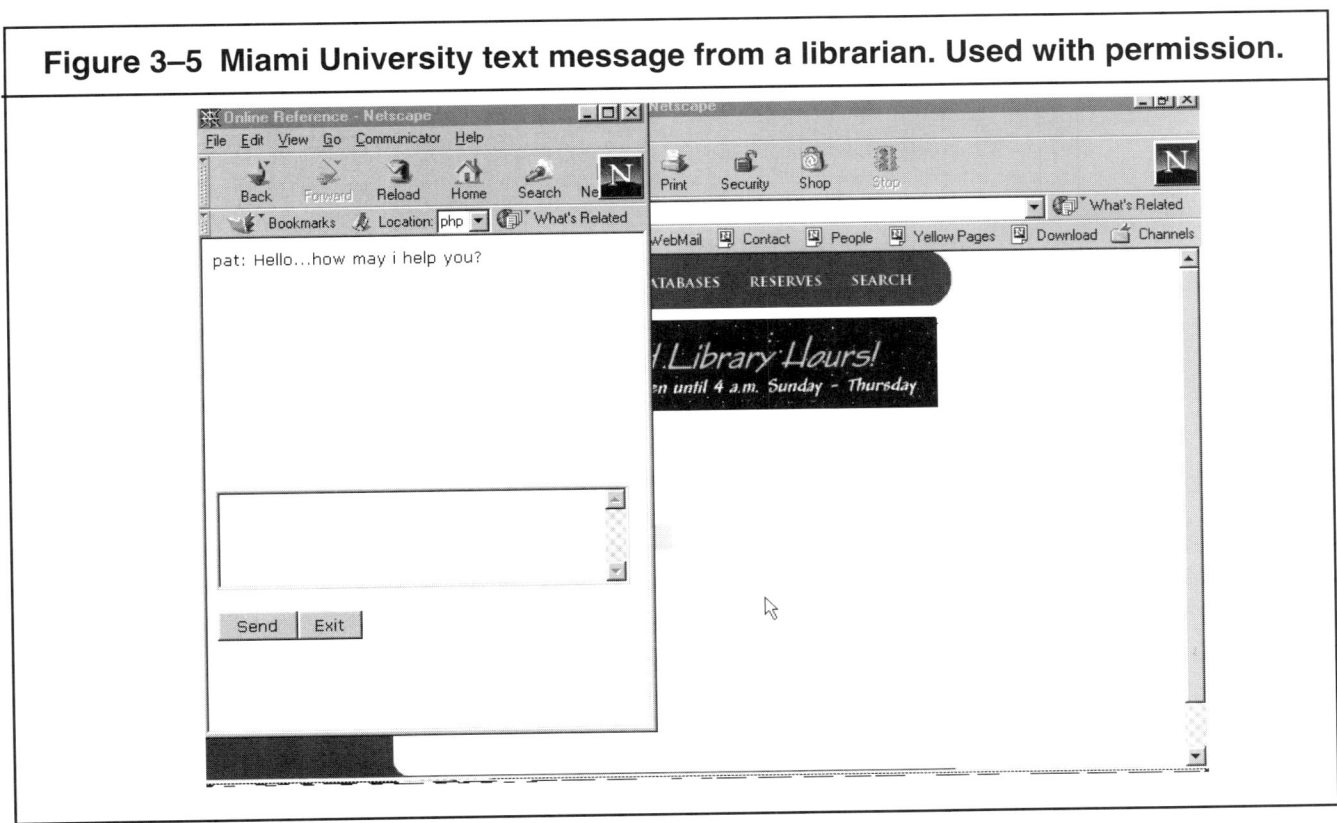

36 STARTING AND OPERATING LIVE VIRTUAL REFERENCE SERVICES

Figure 3–6 Example of Miami University live transaction. Used with permission.

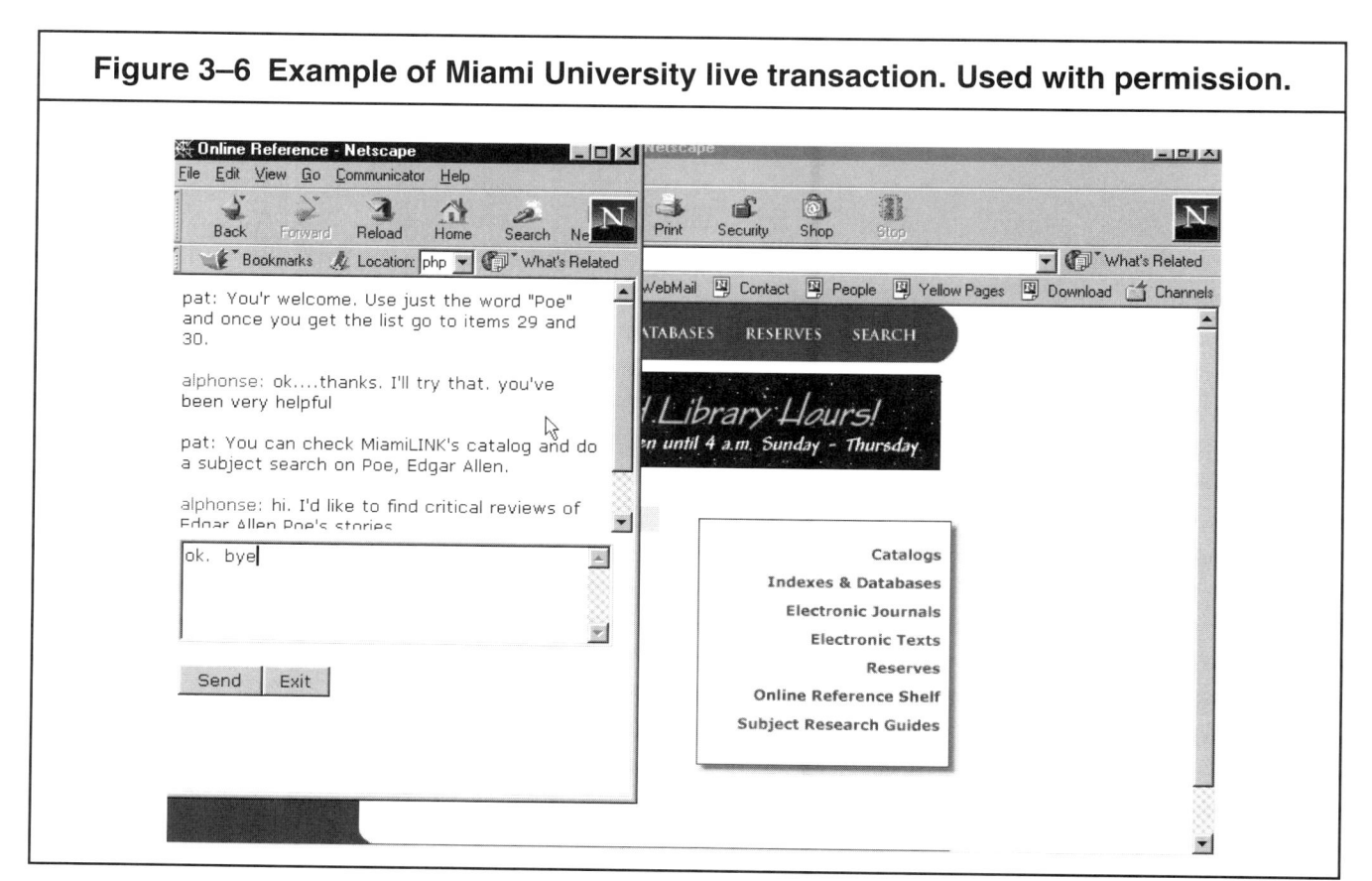

Figure 3–7 Miami University logout screen. Used with permission.

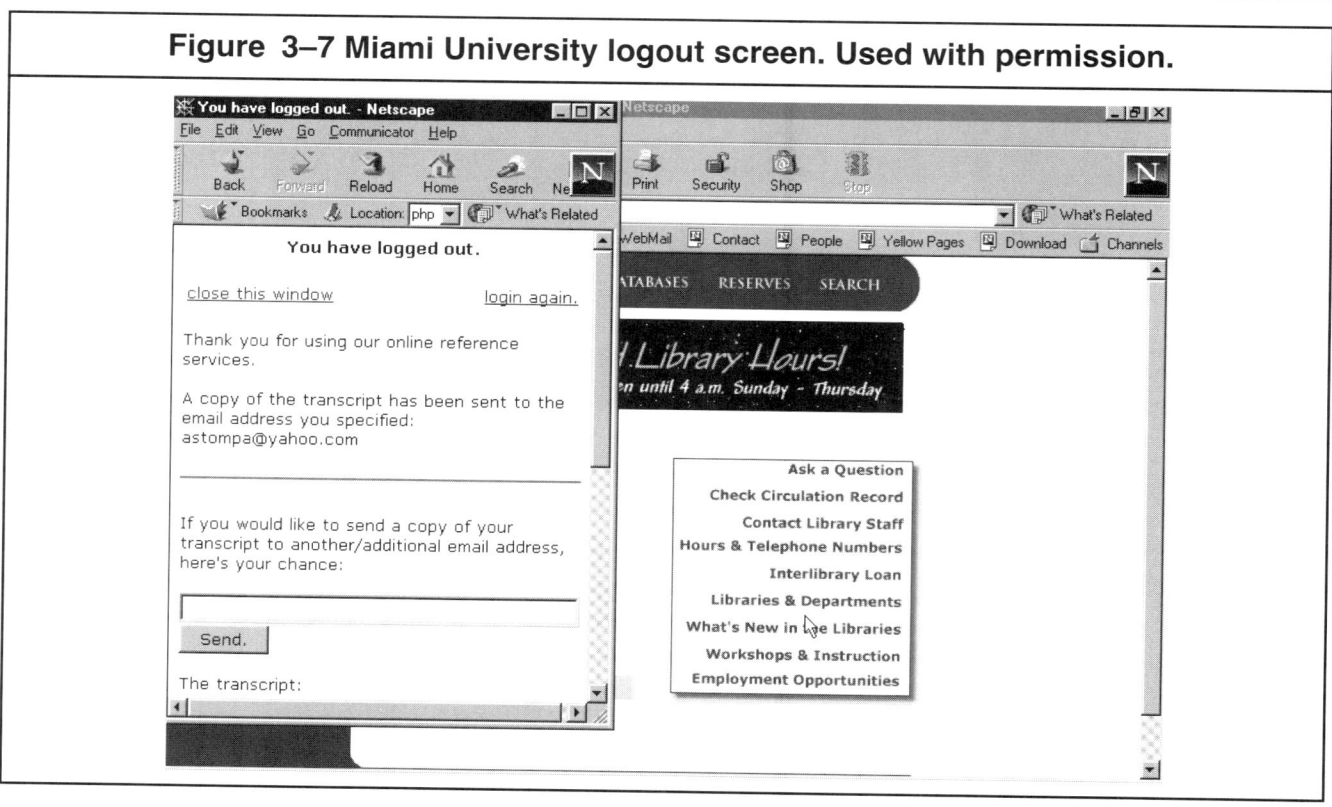

Homegrown Model Summary
• Shares many aspects of basic model • Creates or uses open source software • Software can be customized, may include transcripts and page pushing • Inexpensive • Requires knowledgeable staff to set up and maintain

ADVANCED MODEL—SOPHISTICATED SOFTWARE, SINGLE INSTITUTION

The advanced model is a more complicated way of providing live virtual reference service. In this model, the idea is not simply to offer some version of live text-based chat, but to use interactive features to simulate the physical reference desk transaction as much as possible. In some cases the service may even attempt to go beyond traditional reference service, for example, by being open more hours. The software is expensive, full of features, and may have a longer learning curve for some librarians, especially those with no windows multitasking experience or little experience with chat. Special hardware may be required. Time consuming planning by a large committee with regular meetings can be involved. A grant or budget may have to be obtained. Staffing is usually done away from the physical reference desk, creating the need for an additional virtual desk schedule and additional virtual desk service hours for librarians. The service may have the grand ambition to provide service 24 hours a day, seven days a week, which may possibly involve hiring special staff or outsourcing questions. If the institution offering the service is itself complex, librarians may have to coordinate between different libraries of the same institution. Furthermore, the library may seek to integrate the new service with other services such as in-person reference, e-mail reference, Web page help, and library instruction. Some libraries may begin to question the entire traditional way they provide reference service.

Another way of thinking of the advanced model is to think of libraries that are using expensive, full-featured software but are doing it on their own instead of being involved in collaborative arrangements. Libraries such as MIT and North Carolina State University exemplify the advanced model.

Figure 3–8 shows screenshots of North Carolina State's service. Notice how the patron and librarian can chat in a frame on

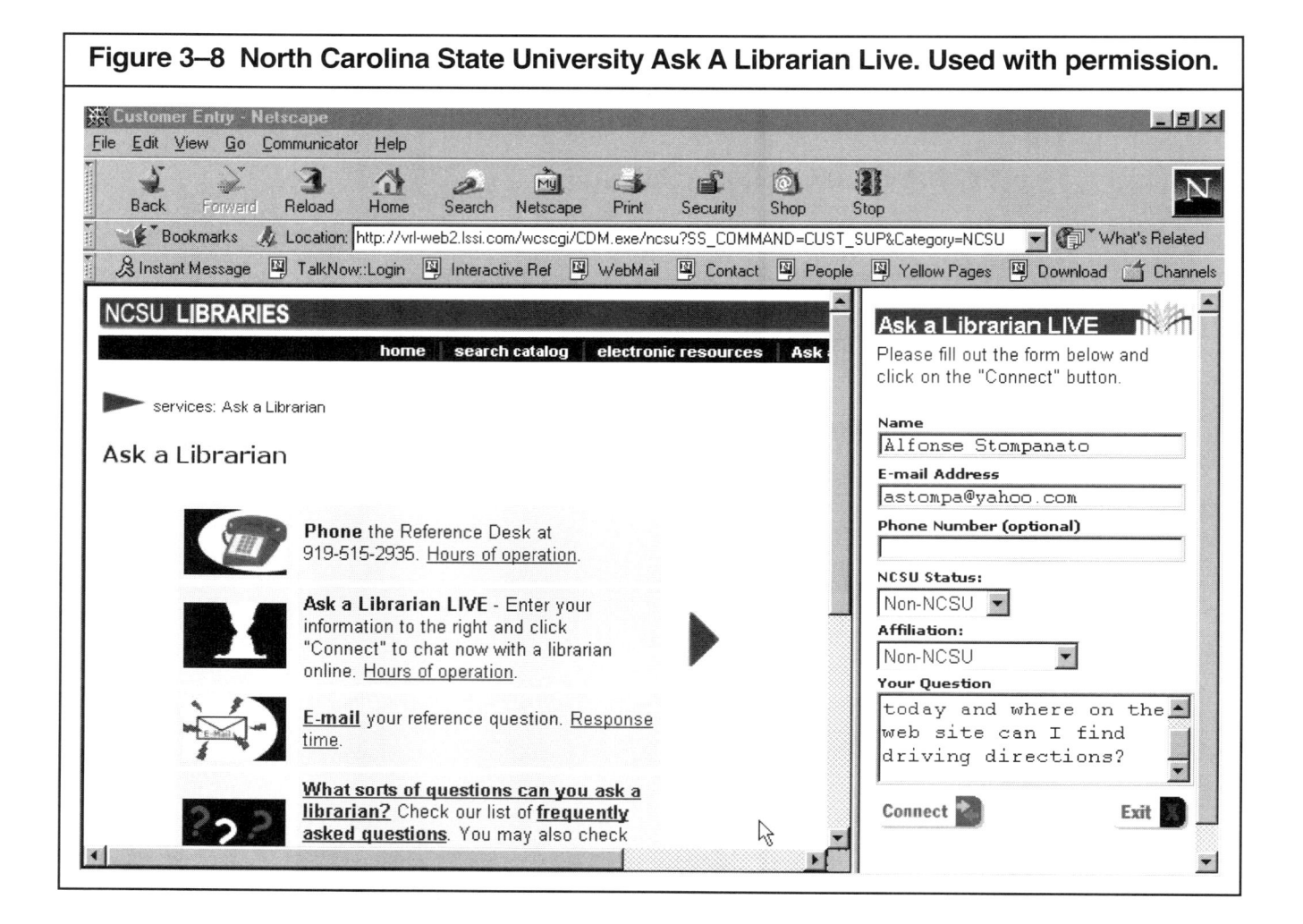

Figure 3–8 North Carolina State University Ask A Librarian Live. Used with permission.

the right-hand side of the page, while the left-hand frame can be used to push Web pages.

Figure 3–9 is an example of page pushing. The patron asked for directions, and the librarian sent a Web page with directions. Page pushing is usually not available in basic or homegrown models.

At the end of the session, the user receives a summary (see Figure 3–10) of the items that were sent in the right-hand frame, in this case the hours and phone numbers, and directions to the library. The patron may then click on these items and revisit them.

Advanced Model
• Chat plus page pushing, transcripts • Expensive • Extensive staff training may be required • May be 24/7 • Large institution or multiple libraries are an additional source of complexity

COLLABORATIVE MODEL—WORKING WITH OTHER LIBRARIES

The collaborative model is really a special case of the advanced model, but it is so important that it merits its own section. In the collaborative model, different libraries come together, usually through a consortium, to share the costs, burdens, and benefits of live virtual reference. This model has so far most frequently been adopted by public libraries. Software used is either Library Systems and Services (LSSI) Virtual Reference Desk or a related package called 24/7 Reference. Grant funding through the Library Services and Technology Act (LSTA) is often used. Planning is extensive, requiring meetings of librarians from different libraries. Training sessions can take place over periods from three to six months. Librarians may have to learn about different institutions in order to answer questions. When libraries collaborate on question answering, staffing arrangements and scheduling are intricate. A consortium may outsource some question answering (especially overnight hours) to independent nonlibrary operators. If hours are 24/7 the goal is to provide live service "anywhere, anytime."

One of the most ambitious collaborative efforts is the Collaborative Digital Reference Service (CDRS) spearheaded by the Library of Congress. CDRS is an international network of libraries that aims to provide anywhere anytime reference service for member libraries. Up to now, the service has been mainly e-mail virtual reference, but plans for live virtual reference are in the works. For more information on CDRS see lcweb.loc.gov/rr/digiref/.

An example of a live virtual reference collaborative model is Q and A NJ, administered by the South Jersey Regional Library Cooperative (SJRLC). SJRLC is a state tax-funded service of the New Jersey Library Network. SJRLC obtained LSTA funds administered by the New Jersey State Library to hire a project leader

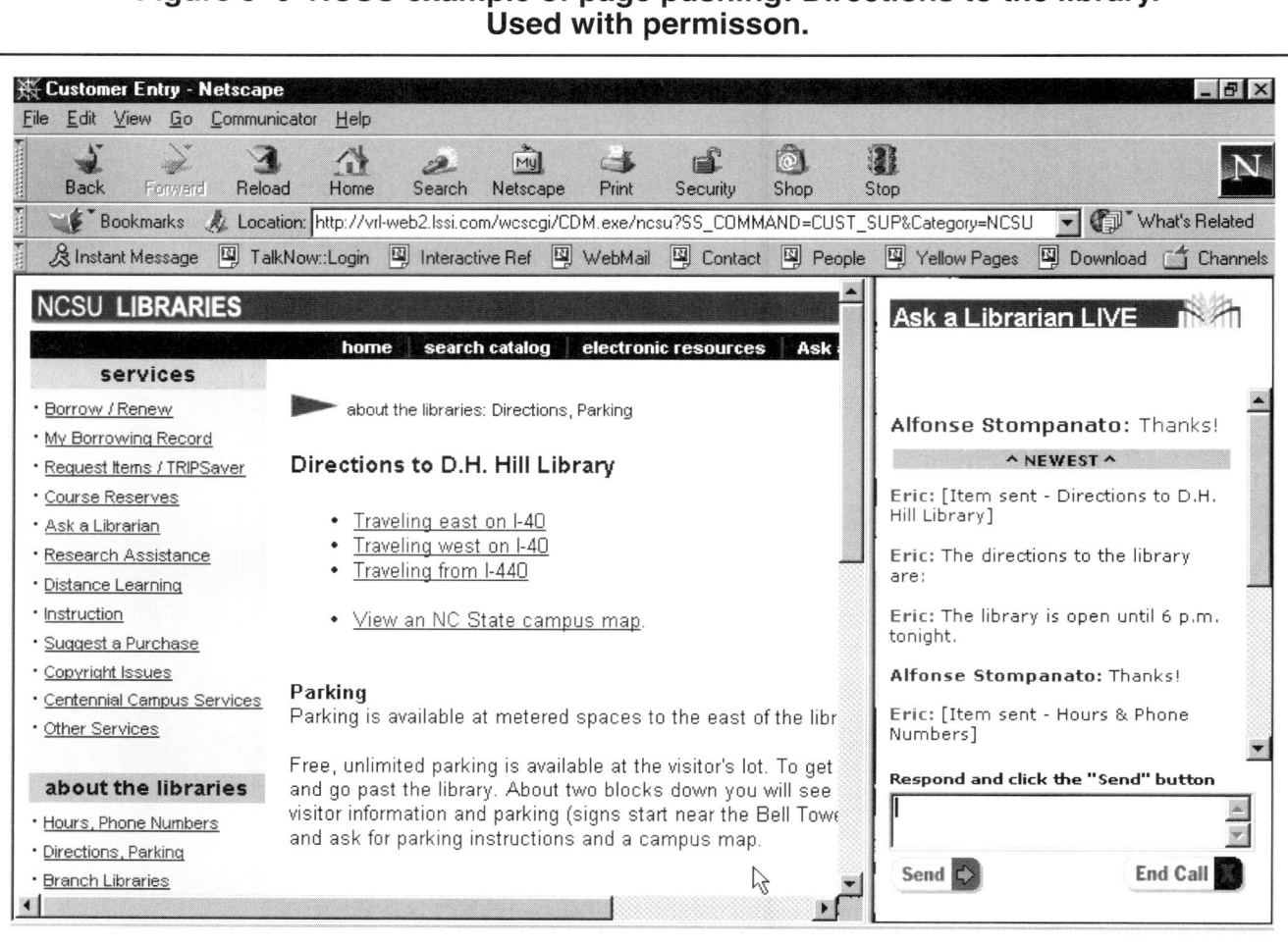

Figure 3–9 NCSU example of page pushing: Directions to the library. Used with permisson.

and purchase LSSI's Virtual Reference Desk software. Through participating member libraries, a special nighttime reference service called NJ Nightline, and librarians from LSSI, Q and A NJ provides residents of New Jersey with live virtual reference service 24 hours a day, seven days a week. Other examples of library consortiums providing live reference include the Metropolitan Cooperative Library System in southern California, the Bay Area Libraries Project in California (Q and A Cafe), the CLEVNET Library Consortium in Ohio, and the Suffolk County Cooperative Library System in New York. Academic library consortiums include the Alliance Library System in Illinois and the Maricopa Community Colleges in Arizona.

Figure 3–11 shows are some screen shots of a sample session

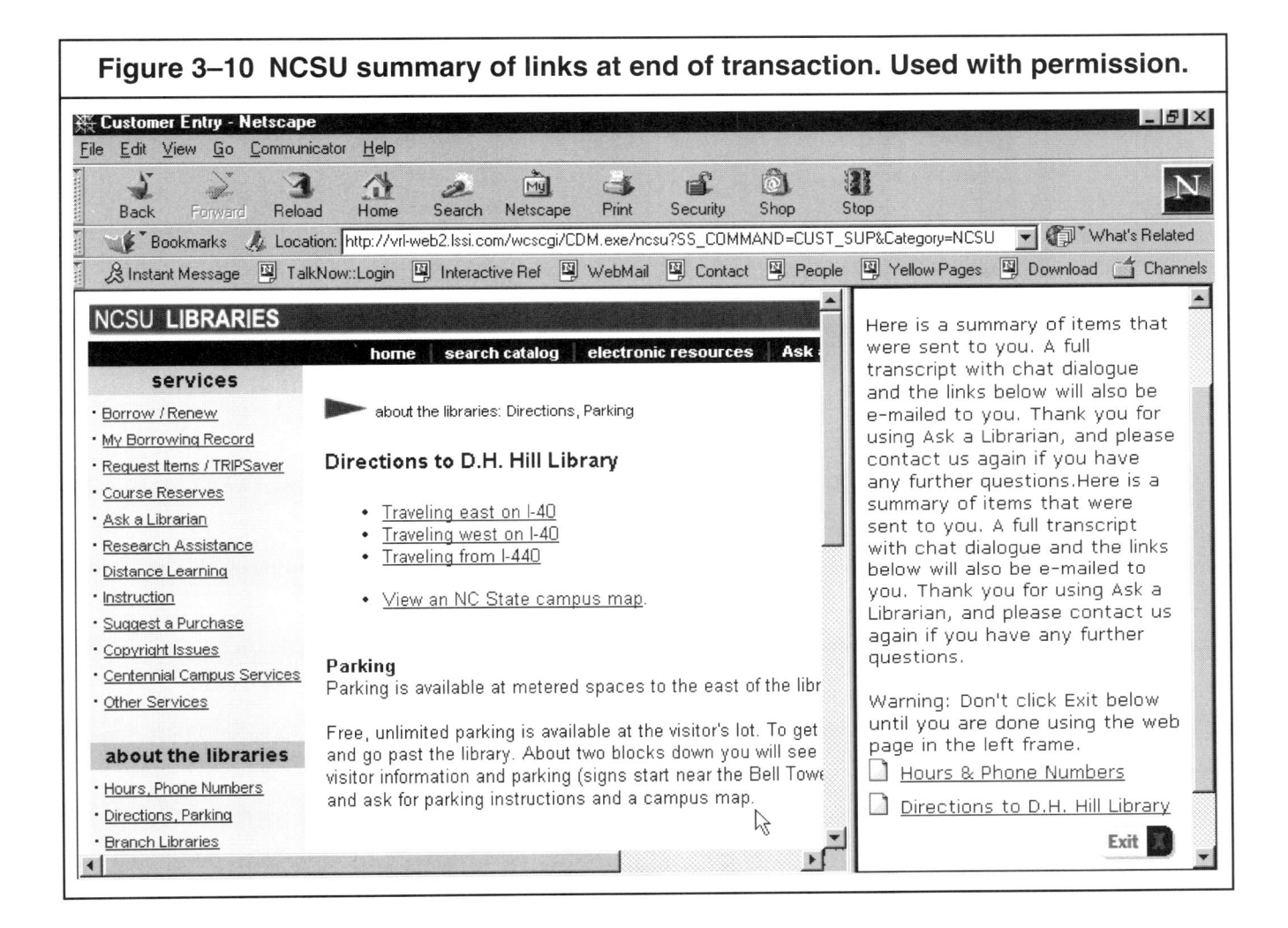

Figure 3–10 NCSU summary of links at end of transaction. Used with permission.

with Q and A NJ. In this example, a simulated patron asks for a speech by Eleanor Roosevelt regarding civil rights. Notice the look of the software is similar to that used by North Carolina State. The patron and librarian chat in the right-hand frame. In the left-hand frame, the patron is offered Web sites to visit while waiting.

In Figure 3–12, the patron receives a Web site that has a speech by Eleanor Roosevelt on civil liberties.

At the end of the session, the patron receives a summary of the links that were pushed by the librarian in the session (see Figure 3–13).

42 STARTING AND OPERATING LIVE VIRTUAL REFERENCE SERVICES

Figure 3–11 Q and A NJ patron submitting a question. Used with permission.

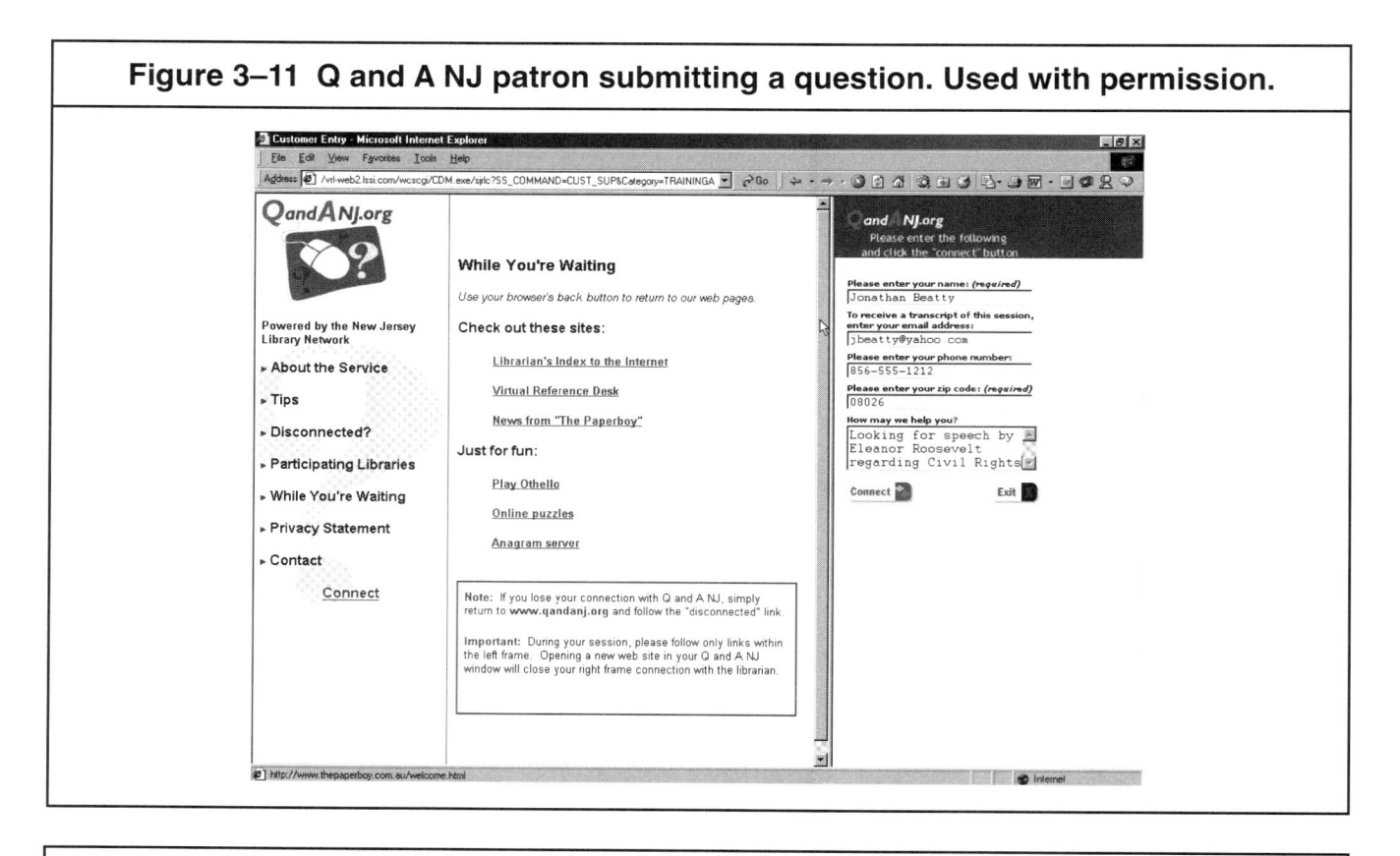

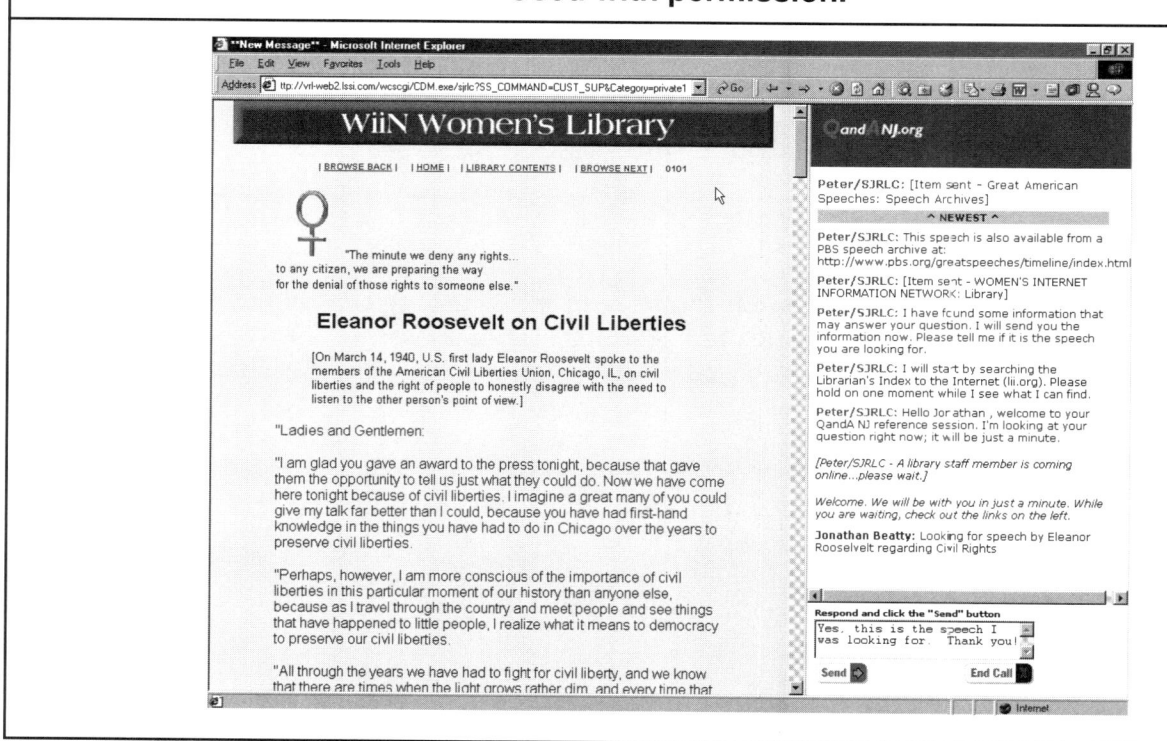

Figure 3–12 Q and A NJ patron receives Web site pushed by librarian. Used with permission.

Figure 3–13 Q and A NJ patron receives summary of links pushed by librarian. Used with permission.

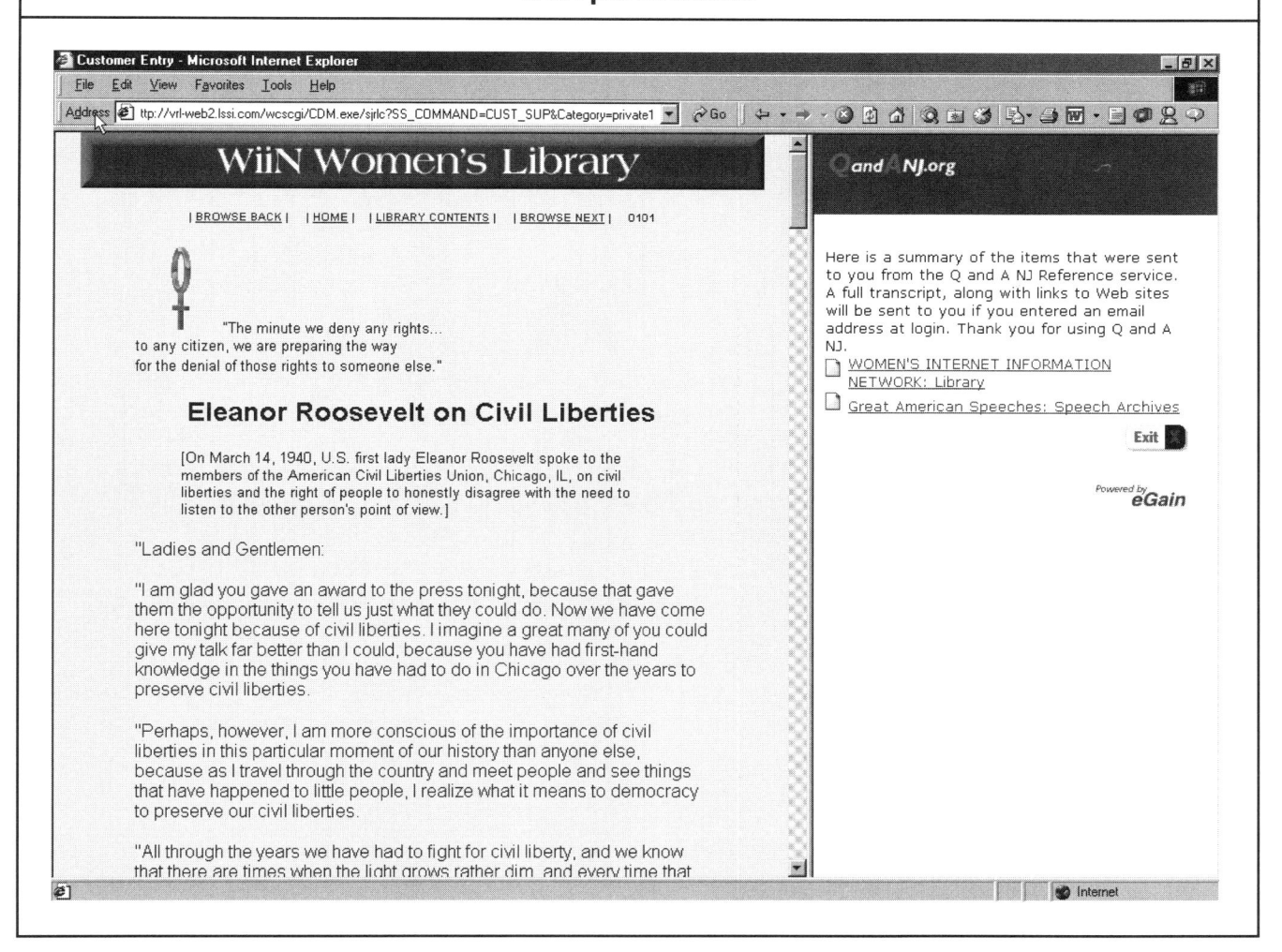

Collaborative Model Summary

- Expensive full-featured software
- Many libraries share costs and benefits
- Most often adopted by public libraries
- Extensive planning and meetings required
- Grant funded
- Intricate staffing arrangements
- Outsourcing of reference work may occur

CORPORATE CALL CENTER MODEL— STAFFING FOR EFFICIENCY AND PROFIT

In addition to looking at what libraries are doing, it is also important to keep up with trends in corporate e-commerce. The practice of live help customer service in e-commerce is important to libraries for a few reasons: it can give you ideas about what is possible and what your users may come to expect; it can illustrate what works and what doesn't; and it can help you keep up with the latest in software, since the corporate demand for software is one of the main drivers of the real-time software market.

Many companies understand that one of the best ways to convince customers who are browsing their Web site to buy their products is to provide live contact with real human beings. A survey by NFO Interactive found that almost 50 percent of people they surveyed would buy more if they could have their questions answered in real-time (Sterne, 2000). Some companies use chat for limited-time promotions of their product. Land O'Lakes, for example, provided live baking help to their customers during April and May of 2001. Customers raved about the immediacy of receiving help from live home economists (PR Newswire, 2001). Webhelp, which previously provided free live help assistance for confused Web surfers, now charges for its service and sells its assistance to companies. Webhelp's client list includes MSN, AOL, Nordic Track, Philips, Norelco, and Netscape.

Two early corporate adopters of live chat that continue to offer live help are Lands' End and 1–800-flowers.com. A study of 1–800-flowers found that answering questions by chat was 30 percent less expensive than e-mail, and that the number of e-mail questions decreased. Operators there said they could respond to four or five chat sessions *simultaneously* (Sterne, 2000). Corporations have reported that chat services are less expensive to operate and generate more revenue for the company than e-mail and telephone customer service (Sterne, 2000). Here's what a live interaction looks like at the Lands' End Web site (Figures 3–14 to 3–18). On the "contact us" page (Figure 3–14), customers are given a choice of ways to contact the company, phone, e-mail, fax, mail, and live chat.

After clicking on the Lands' End Live link, the customer is given a further choice between talking to a representative by phone (which requires a second phone line or direct connection to the Internet) or by text chat (Figure 3–15). This is something we haven't seen on any library site: the suggestion is that the cus-

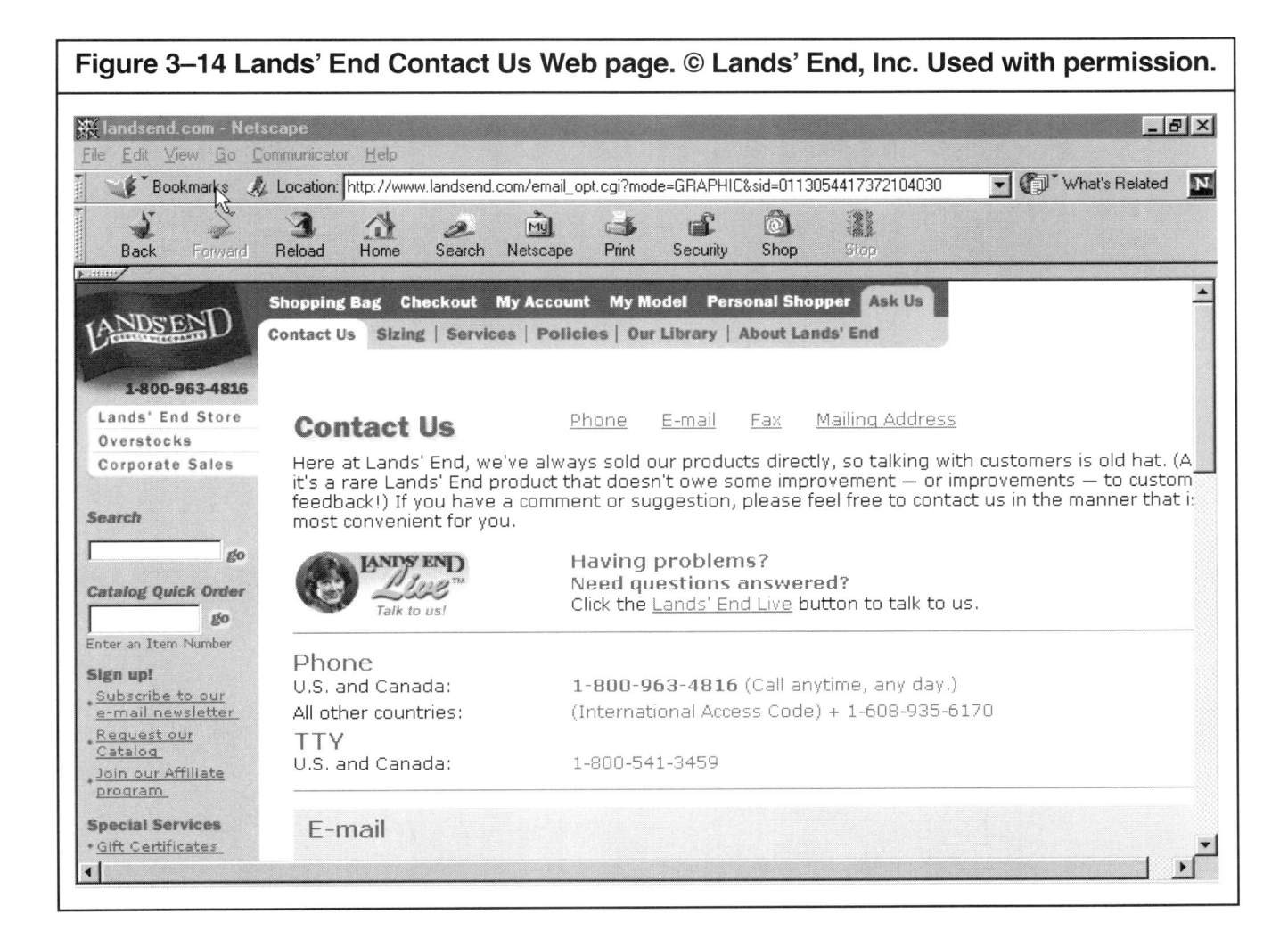

Figure 3–14 Lands' End Contact Us Web page. © Lands' End, Inc. Used with permission.

tomer can receive a call back from a customer service representative by phone while browsing the Web site.

After selecting chat, and clicking on connect, a text chat window pops up (Figure 3–16). Notice the first message from the representative: "Welcome to Lands' End Live! How may I help you?" This is the kind of message that can be scripted, saving the agent typing time.

The customer can now type and receive messages. We used the pseudonym "James Sheldon" to ask if Lands' End chinos come in a lighter type of material for spring and summer (Figure 3–17). The Lands' End representative told us that Lands' End chinos are the same weight year round. But the representative took the opportunity to mention poplin pants. This is known as cross selling. If the store doesn't have an item the customer is looking for, the salesperson informs the customer of another item that

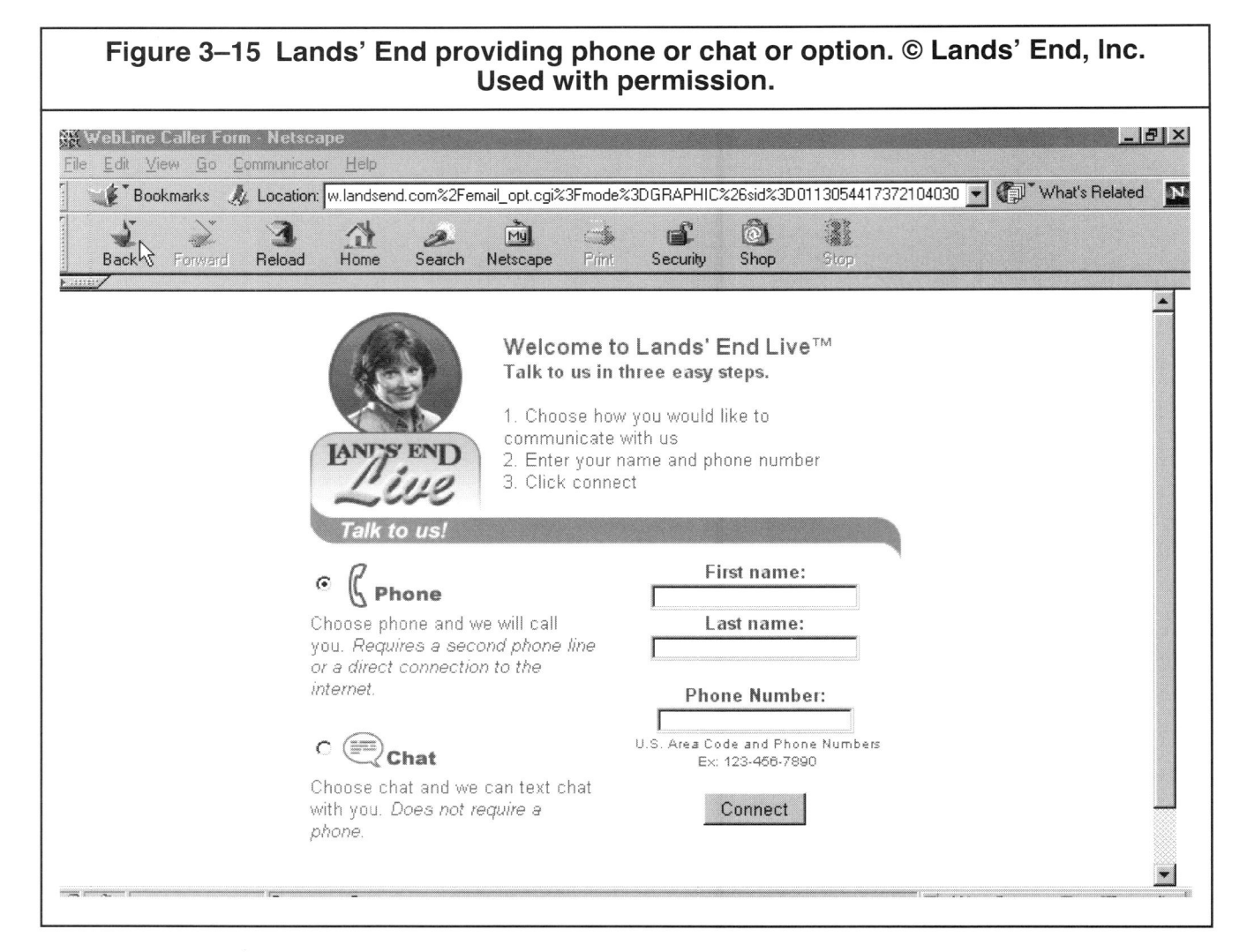

Figure 3–15 Lands' End providing phone or chat or option. © Lands' End, Inc. Used with permission.

might be of interest. Librarians, of course, are aware of this strategy. A patron may come in looking for a magazine, but if the library doesn't have it, a librarian may suggest an alternative, perhaps a full-text newspaper database. This is what live interactivity is all about. Instead of someone leaving your Web site dissatisfied, they have learned about a new resource. In this case, we asked the Lands' End rep to show us what poplin pants look like, and the rep pushed us the Web page from the catalog. We decided that poplin pants are perfect for summer days at the reference desk, so we ordered some!

To close the call, the customer receives a "thank you for participating" Web page (Figure 3–18).

Companies are similar to libraries in that many strive to provide high-quality customer service to their clients and customers.

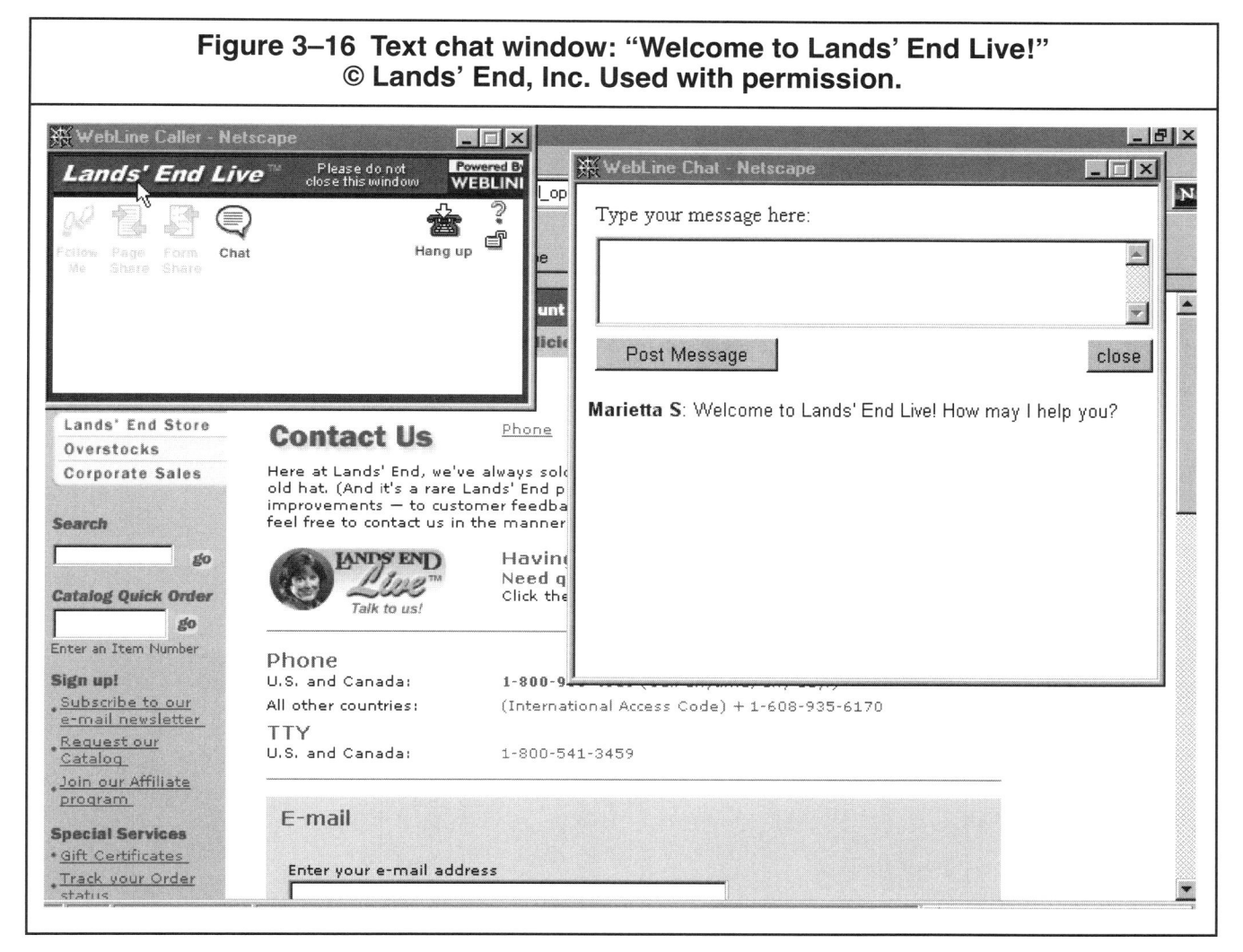

Figure 3–16 Text chat window: "Welcome to Lands' End Live!"
© Lands' End, Inc. Used with permission.

The success of their business often depends on it. Because they are focused on profitability, however, companies are usually interested in the most efficient and cost-effective customer service solution. Companies use frequently asked questions (FAQs), lists, bulletin boards, and self-help Web pages to deflect questions from their live operators. One difference between corporate customer service and library reference service may be that companies can expect their questions to fall within a narrower range and be more predictable than questions received in a library. The more that questions are predictable and are able to be categorized, the more chance there is that answers can be automated. Although our definition of live virtual reference specifies human help, automated machine help is attractive to organizations that have a high volume of repetitive questions. Coca-Cola, Ford, and Oracle for ex-

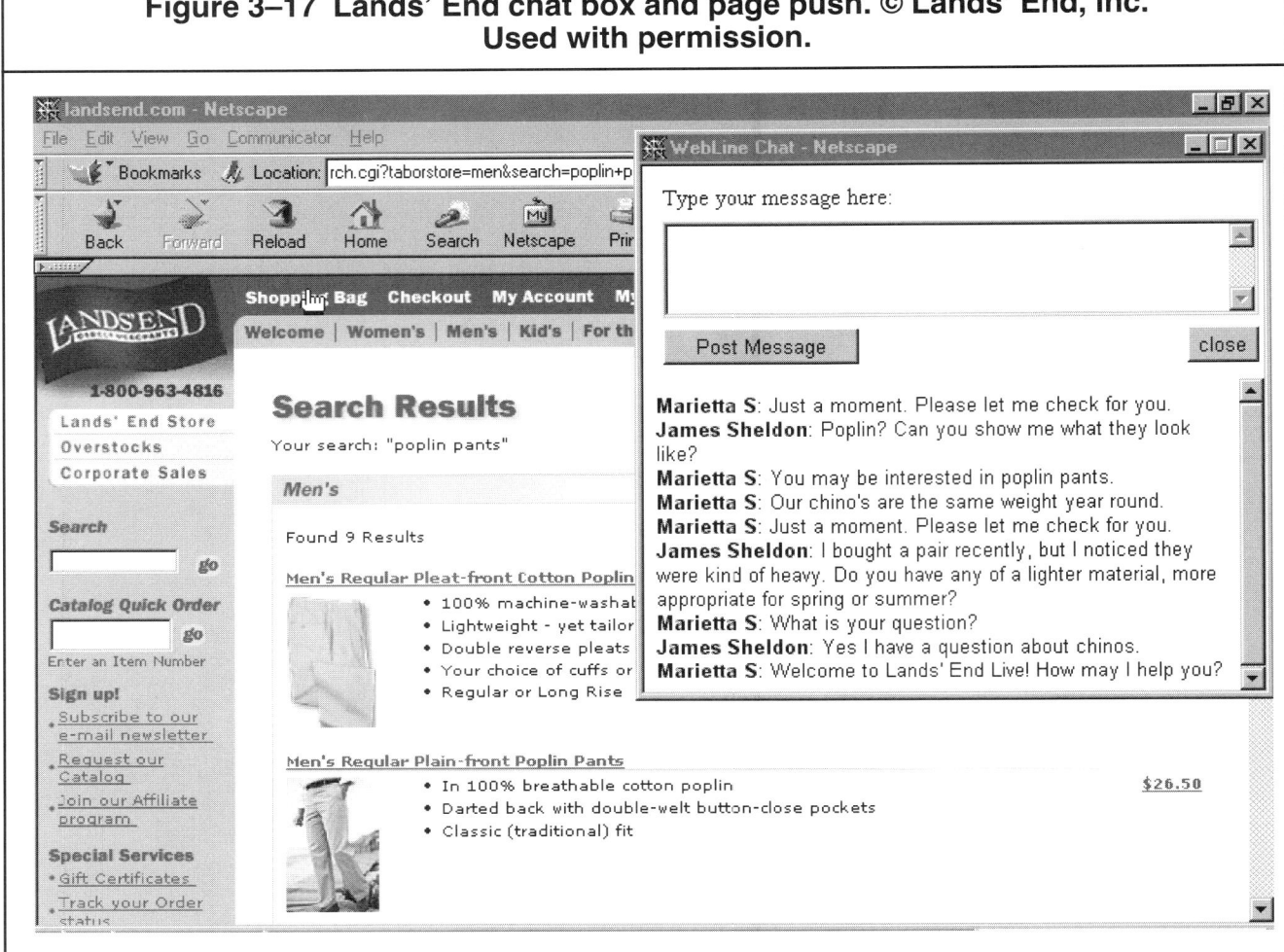

Figure 3–17 Lands' End chat box and page push. © Lands' End, Inc. Used with permission.

ample, are using a new type of software technology called vRep, short for virtual representative (Chartrand, 2001). The vRep is a photograph or animated image on a Web page that answers customer questions in real-time using a database of stored answers. Whether this way of providing customer service will affect libraries remains to be seen. Most libraries report receiving such a wide range of questions that this type of automation will be difficult to put into practice (Sloan, 2001).

How far should libraries go in emulating the corporate call center model? Coffman and Saxton have argued (1999) that adopting a call center model could "revolutionize" reference by centralizing staffing, increasing efficiency, and reducing staffing needs. They asserted that many reference questions could be answered by paraprofessionals, and that professional reference staff

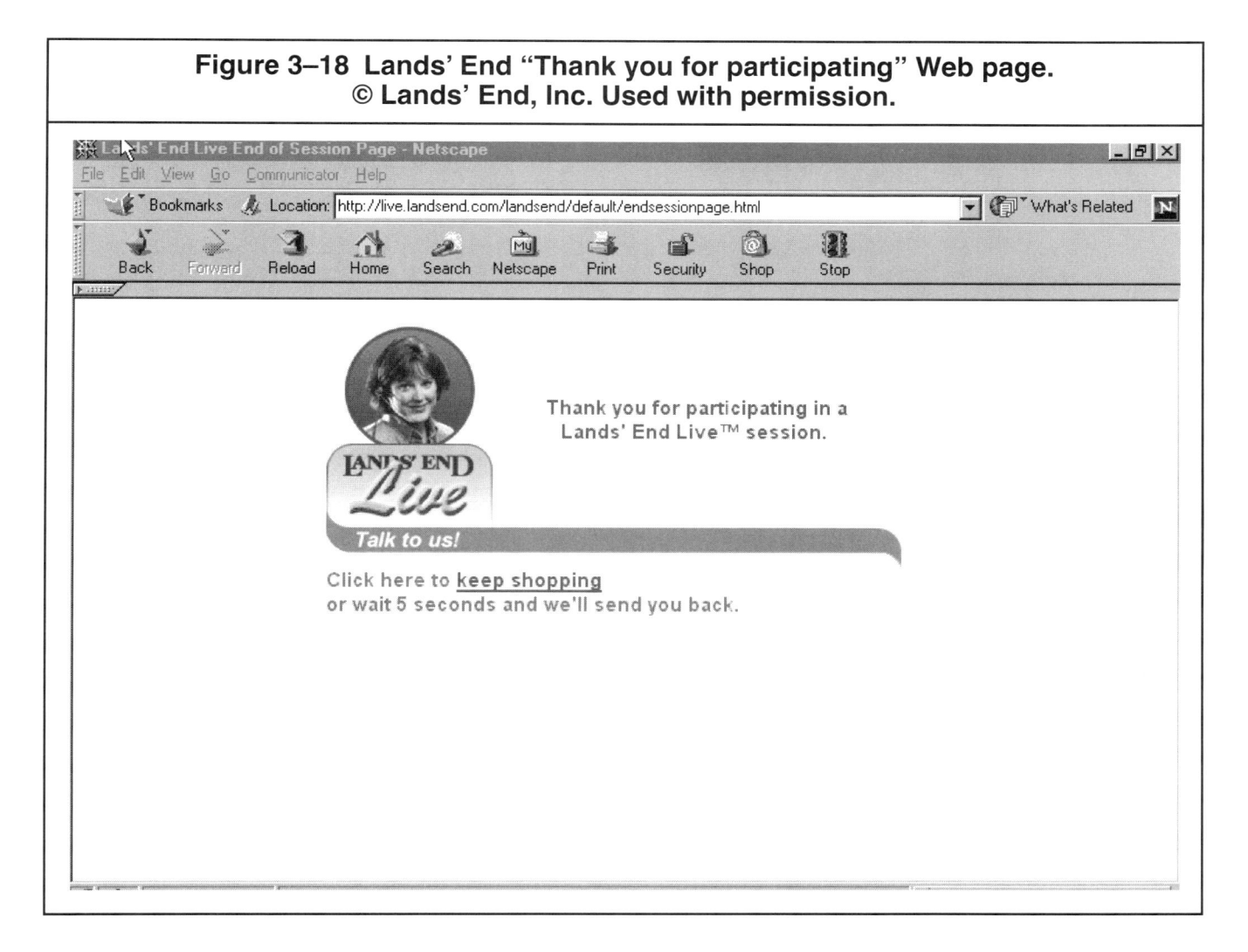

**Figure 3–18 Lands' End "Thank you for participating" Web page.
© Lands' End, Inc. Used with permission.**

could be reduced by "42% or more" at the County of Los Angeles Public Library by predicting the number of staff needed to answer a given volume of calls at a given time (1999: 153).

These ideas don't sit well with many librarians. Dilevko has warned (2001) against applying the corporate call center model to libraries claiming instead that it will lead to deprofessionalization, increased automation, and lack of career opportunities for librarians. Library directors who embrace digital reference call centers, Dilevko says, ignore the negative aspects of call centers in their drive to apply new technology and cut costs (2001: 218).

Fortunately, we believe that one does not have to adopt the corporate call center model and its negative aspects to implement a live virtual reference service. Our belief is that live virtual refer-

Summary of Corporate Call Center Model
• Focused on efficiency and cost effectiveness • Corporate values may clash with library values • Call queuing and distribution • Automated answers and knowledge bases

ence can fit into a traditional model of reference service in which technology is used as a tool to provide high-quality, personalized human help by real, live human librarians. Be aware of the corporate model, but be careful to steer clear of the Scylla of its negative consequences, while avoiding the Charybdis of sitting at the traditional reference desk while questions decline and the Internet passes libraries by.

SUMMARY

There is more than one way to implement live virtual reference. A legitimate, serviceable live virtual reference model can be put into practice for not much cost and in not very much time. The low-budget bare-bones approach can work fine for libraries with limited means or modest goals. A simple live reference service using free or close to free software can achieve a lot by helping users quickly in real-time and getting librarians accustomed to communicating by Internet chat. Larger libraries with more caller volume will have difficulty, however, staffing live virtual reference simultaneously with in-person reference at a physical reference desk. To handle more calls it will be necessary to separate the live virtual reference from the physical reference desk. In addition, to go beyond quick, simple answers to relatively simple questions, librarians will want to acquire live virtual reference software with more sophisticated features. Software with more sophisticated features means either spending more time developing a homegrown solution, or spending more money on an advanced software package. To share costs, and to share the burden of staffing a second desk, librarians have begun to do something new: collaborate on answering reference questions. In the background to all this library activity is the corporate sector, which has devised its own ways of serving virtual customers. Which model is best for your library? Current practice suggests that most academic libraries are using free or modestly priced software, and a significant minority are using advanced software. Most public libraries, on the other hand, are participating in collaborative models that use expensive sophisticated software that is funded through grants administered through consortiums. Are these models and choices set in stone? No. These models and variations on them will no doubt give way to new models. Keeping one eye on the practices and software coming out of the corporate call center is a good way to look for new ideas; keeping one eye on traditional library values will ensure that the standards of the past will continue to inform the reference librarianship of the future.

REFERENCES

Chartrand, Sabra. 2001. Software to Provide "Personal" Attention to Online Customers with Service Untouched by a Human. New York Times, Monday, late edition.

Coffman, Steve, and Matthew L. Saxton. 1999. "Staffing the Reference Desk in the Largely-Digital Library." *The Reference Librarian* 66: 141–163.

Dilevko, Juris. 2001. "An Ideological Analysis of Digital Reference Service Models." *Library Trends* 2 (Fall): 218–244.

Fagan, Jody Condit, and Michele Calloway. 2001. "Creating an Instant Messaging Reference System." *Information Technology and Libraries*. 20:4 [Online]. Available: www.lita.org/ital/ital2004.html#anchor250046 [2002, April 29].

PR Newswire. March 20, 2001. Lexis Nexis [2002, April 29].

Sloan, Bernie. 2001. Ready for Reference: Academic Libraries Offer Live Web-Based Reference Evaluating System Use. www.lis.uiuc.edu/~b-sloan/r4r.final.htm.

Sterne, Jim. 2000. *Customer Service on the Internet*. 2nd Edition. Boston: John Wiley and Sons.

PART II

PREPARING FOR LIVE VIRTUAL REFERENCE

4 PLANNING FOR LIVE VIRTUAL REFERENCE—A NINE-STEP PROCESS

You now should have a clearer idea of what live virtual reference is, why you should or shouldn't do it, and what some of the different models of service look like. The next step toward bringing live virtual reference to your institution is to start planning. The nature of the planning process will vary depending on your institution and on which model of live virtual reference you ultimately choose, but the essential steps should include: articulate a vision, form a committee, gather information, investigate funding, decide on staffing, select software, make choices about policy, implement and evaluate the service once it's up and running. Whatever model of live virtual reference you choose, this work has to get done for your project to be successful. The following is an overview of the entire process. Many of the key steps are explained in full in later chapters.

STEP 1: ARTICULATE A VISION

Whether you are a librarian who wants to propose live virtual reference to your director, a director who wants to impose live virtual reference on your librarians, or a librarian who wants to convince other librarians of the value of live virtual reference, it helps if you have a clear notion of what you want your live virtual reference service to do, why you want to do it, and how you will fit it into existing services. Live virtual reference takes five fundamental forms. The idea behind the basic model is to communicate with patrons in real-time with simple software, simple staffing, and low cost. The adopter of the homegrown model believes that a functional real-time reference service can be provided without paying for expensive software. The vision behind the more advanced and collaborative models involves more features, more cost, and greater complexity in staffing. The corporate model tries to provide customer service and increase sales on the Web with maximum efficiency. Articulating a vision is important because it affects what software you choose, what hours you operate your service, how much time and money you spend on it, and how you staff it.

When we began to articulate our vision of live virtual reference at Temple in the late 1990s, simplicity was a driving force. Our early vision had two components: one, our beliefs about our users' needs and capabilities, and two, our small (nonexistent) budget. Our vision of the service was a quick way for mystified users to get immediate answers to their questions. We believed that the declining number of questions at the physical reference desk were not a true indication of how many users didn't understand how to use the library effectively. We received enough questions at the desk from people who were completely clueless that we strongly believed there had to be many more clueless people out there. They just didn't bother coming in to the desk or didn't know how to ask a question. We wanted to reach these people. This was important in determining what software we would use. Because we assumed the people contacting us would be having troubles in their information research, we wanted the software they used to contact us to be as easy as possible. We didn't want to have to teach them how to use the program to contact us in addition to having to teach them how to use the online catalog or how to search a database. Since we also knew that librarians had enough new interfaces to learn, we wanted the software to be ultra-simple on their end as well. In addition, we did not have much of a budget for the project, so we wanted the software to be free or of very low cost. Our belief in simplicity led us to envision at first a basic model of service, and then later to a homegrown model.

Other libraries have been driven by other factors. North Carolina State University realized that since many of their resources were on the Web, their reference librarians also needed to be on the Web. Their institution has large numbers of distance learners and a number of geographically dispersed campuses and libraries. Their university also has a tradition of experimenting with technology (Boyer 2001). North Carolina State decided to choose a more expensive software package with sophisticated page pushing and co-browsing features. Page pushing and co-browsing allow the librarian to escort the patron around the Web, showing as well as telling the patron where to go. In terms of staffing, NCSU already had a separate reference desk set up for phone and e-mail questions, so adding live virtual reference was natural (Boyer 2001). The advanced model of live virtual reference fit NCSU's situation well.

The Cleveland Public Library needed to articulate a different vision for the CLEVNET consortium. Bob Carterette described

> **Articulate a Vision Checklist**
>
> —What do you want your service to accomplish?
>   Quick simple answers
>   Real-time chat
>   Page-pushing and co-browsing
>   24/7 availability
> —Why?
>   User need
>   Serve distance learners
>   Develop librarian skills
>   Keep pace with technology
> —How will you get it done?
>   Free software
>   Homegrown solution
>   Institutional budget
>   Grant funding
>   Collaborate with others

that from the beginning, they wanted to offer a live virtual reference service that had 24/7 hours of operation. Problem: they didn't have the staff to maintain these hours. Solution: an advanced collaborative staffing arrangement that had Cleveland Public Library librarians staffing the service, combined with consortium member librarians, combined with overnight staff contracted from LSSI. Their vision of a 24/7 service drove the choices they made about software and staffing.

Articulating a vision can be facilitated by examining your beliefs, analyzing your situation, looking at what others are doing, and imagining what is possible from what software is available. Look at your institution's mission, budget, staff, your perception of your users' needs, and the services you are currently offering. A clear vision that is grounded in current reality will help you make the important decisions that shape your live virtual reference service.

STEP 2: FORM A COMMITTEE

The formal structure of a committee, a task force, or a working group that has meetings, generates minutes, and produces reports has an important role to play in the planning process. Libraries of all sizes will need some formality and structure to divide the workload, generate consensus, and maintain communication. Large libraries and consortia will need it even more. By dividing up the work, a larger committee can keep tasks on track and maintain forward progress where a small team might be slowed down if one or two individuals get sidetracked by other responsibilities.

The number of members on a committee can vary. The more interested members the better. You can even begin the process with as few as two. At Temple, we started our live virtual reference planning with a committee of two. This caused problems later on when one of us first took on new responsibilities, then left for another job, and the other had less time to devote to the day-to-day management of the service. Having a large committee helps maintain continuity.

Hold regular committee meetings, then involve key stakeholders in the decision making process. This builds support for the project, heads off potential objections, and provides a forum for your creative staff members to contribute their good ideas. Making sure everyone has input makes the service better and makes people feel better at the same time. Participants will care more about the project if they have been consulted and their concerns have been addressed. A committee can also comfort those who are nervous about rapid change. Instead of diving in and acting quickly, many committees start slowly with some form of survey or study. This gives the committee time to ruminate, and gives a degree of control over the situation or at least the illusion of it. Consensus building is one of the main tasks that can get accomplished through a committee.

In our experience at Temple, consensus was an area that suffered. We didn't have a formal committee, and although we solicited feedback about the service, a more proactive approach would have been more successful. The working group for live reference at UCLA, for example, had weekly meetings to discuss software, interface with developers, and improve librarian chat skills. They also used meetings to develop procedures, scripts, and bookmarks.

In the collaborative model, communication with members is even more important. For example, the 30 library systems of the CLEVNET consortium went from planning to implementation in less than six months. How did they do this? CLEVNET set up six working groups: training, standards and guidelines, implementation, evaluation, coordination, and an executive group. Each had a specific charge and a timeline to follow, working backward from a deadline. Members of the working groups were drawn from the consortium membership to ensure broad input and participation. Bob Carterette of Cleveland Public Library maintains that giving everyone a chance to voice their concerns was essential to the success of the project.

Although CLEVNET reaped the advantages of the large committee approach in organization and consensus building, they did not sacrifice openness or flexibility. Working groups were encouraged from the outset to be flexible and not attempt to solve all problems, in part because they had no way of knowing what problems would come up. Standards and guidelines were left open but at the same time were built on the broad base of experience that had been acquired by CLEVNET's reference librarians over the years. By having a firm structure while also maintaining flexibility, CLEVNET was able to bring their service up quickly.

STEP 3: GATHER INFORMATION

The process of gathering information is critical. It will help you and your committee define and refine your vision, identify available software, and make better decisions about policy. You'll need to gather information on other libraries that have implemented live virtual reference and how they've done it. You'll need to identify software packages and their pricing models. You'll need to assess your own internal situation to gauge your readiness for live virtual reference. Some of this work can be done on the World Wide Web, some by telephone interviews, some through reading articles or conducting surveys, some through listservs and conferences. We devote a full chapter to the best ways to gather information in Chapter 5.

STEP 4: INVESTIGATE FUNDING

The availability of funding will impact your service model. If no funding is available, you may have to go with a basic or homegrown model out of necessity. If money is not a problem, you will be able to afford an advanced software package and possibly expand your hours. Investigating the possibility of securing funding is an important job for the planning committee.

There are at least three routes that your committee needs to investigate: internal funding, external funding, and collaboration with a consortium. Internal funding could start with something as simple as setting up a meeting with your director, but most likely will involve submitting a formal budget request with detailed information. One possible source of internal money is re-allocating existing funds from operating or materials budgets. You may be able to argue that live virtual reference warrants a re-evaluation of existing priorities. External funding will of course involve even more detailed proposal writing. One source of grant money that has been used in the past for live virtual reference has been the Library Services and Technology Act (LSTA). LSTA grants are administered through the State Library in your state. For more information on LSTA grants see the Institute of Museum and Library Services Web page at www.imls.gov/grants/library/lib_gsla.asp. Yet another possibility is pooling resources with a consortium in your region. Consortiums may be able to negotiate deals with software vendors, just as they do with subscription databases.

STEP 5: DECIDE ON STAFFING

Deciding on how your live virtual reference service will be staffed is a crucial planning issue. The most important question in terms of staffing is who will answer questions. In deciding who will answer questions, you need to decide not only who will answer but where and when will questions be answered. Depending on how you decide to answer questions, you may also have to decide if you will route questions to subject specialists or filter out inappropriate questions. After questions have been answered, someone has to evaluate the quality of the answers. You should be ready to encounter some staff opposition from librarians who are uncomfortable with new technology and unhappy about having their answers evaluated. Techniques you can use to deal with this include staff training and staffing by volunteers. Staffing and training are topics that will be treated thoroughly in Chapters 6 and 9.

STEP 6: SELECT SOFTWARE

Software, of course, is another major issue. Since software is constantly changing, your planning team will need to come up with a list of desirable features and then identify the main packages, their prices, advantages, and disadvantages. Set up trials with the different packages and test them. If you are considering open source software, you need to find programmers or system administrators who are capable of setting the system up. See Chapter 7 for a discussion of the leading available software packages.

STEP 7: DRAFT POLICY

After deciding the staffing and software issues, begin drafting policy. This is one area in which you can draw on your existing policies, especially if you already operate an e-mail virtual reference service. Your live virtual reference policy should be a natural extension of your existing policies. You can stay as close as possible to your existing policies at first, then adjust if you need to. Later, you may have to change your long-existing reference policies because live virtual reference has caused you to rethink how you provide service. Initially, three areas of policy need particular attention: audience, level of service, and privacy.

AUDIENCE

Who is the audience for the service? Will you accept questions from the entire world, or just your user community? How will you define and limit access to your user community? If your current audience for your in-person service is limited, limit your virtual service in a similar way. Later, if you want to receive more questions, open up access to more people. If you want to reduce your questions, limit your audience or restrict the hours. Librarians are often nervous about being deluged by questions and may be soothed if users will be restricted in some way. Public libraries can limit users by zip code, academic libraries can limit by e-mail addresses or proxy authentication. It's true that wily patrons can get usually get around these limitations (by entering a fake zip code for example), but if you don't market your service to users in other states chances are they aren't going to find out about you. Academic libraries have not been overwhelmed by answering questions of their primary user community, plus any questions that pertain specifically to their library collection.

LEVEL OF SERVICE

Another policy question is determining what level of service you will provide. How long a period of time should reference librarians spend on questions? Should librarians teach search strategies or provide answers? Will document delivery be available and how does this relate to your current database licenses? What resources should librarians use—print and electronic or electronic only? Library databases or Internet only? What are the service hours? Time spent on questions can be left up to the judgment of librarians, but if you want you can set a general guideline of 15 to 20 minutes a question. If you are an academic library, traditionally you focus on teaching strategies over providing answers, and you can do the same in your live service. Public libraries typically provide answers; your live service can be similar. For simplicity's sake, you can start out staying away from document delivery, but if your library normally offers some kind of document delivery you may want to decide how to integrate that into your live service. The longer your service hours are, the better for your users, but obviously you will need staff to cover these hours. Try to match your physical desk hours as closely as possible.

PRIVACY

Protecting the privacy and confidentiality of library users is an important part of library service. The American Library Association's Code of Ethics states that librarians "...protect each library user's right to privacy and confidentiality with respect to information sought or received and resources consulted, borrowed, acquired or transmitted" (ALA Code of Ethics, Revised 1995). Previously, patron privacy was mostly the problem of the circulation department, since it was here that records were kept of which materials patrons had checked out of the library. But respecting a user's right to privacy is a traditional library value that surely needs to be preserved in the virtual library.

In the virtual environment, polls and reports continue to indicate users are very concerned about online privacy (Thibodeau, 2002; Pew, 2000). Text-based live virtual reference presents more opportunities than ever before for reference librarians to gather information about who reference patrons are, what kinds of questions they are asking, and what kind of answers they are receiving. At the traditional physical library reference desk, seldom is there a written record of patron queries and librarian answers. In live virtual reference, however, patron names, e-mail addresses, phone numbers, and transcripts of entire reference interactions can be recorded and archived. Some live virtual reference software enables you to compile a kind of dossier on patrons, so that when a patron asks a question, you can click on their name and see all the previous reference questions they have asked. Although this may sound like an exciting new way to tailor service, it is important to think through the privacy implications. Decide what your privacy policy is and post it on your Web site. Use the following questions to guide your thinking on your privacy policy. Will you require patrons to enter their names and e-mail addresses? Will transcripts of patron-librarian interactions be created and stored? Will you use the transcripts for training purposes? Will you evaluate librarian performance based on them? Will you sell them to a marketing company? Will you show them to the FBI if they ask you to? How long will transcripts be kept? If they are to be deleted, who will delete them and on what schedule? If you are using a service hosted on a remote server, can you trust that your patron's privacy will be preserved by the vendor?

A safe way to begin is to maintain very conservative privacy standards. Give the patron as much choice as possible in whether or not to reveal identifying information. If you do store information and use it for training purposes, strip out personal information that could be used to identify an individual. Keep statistics in the aggregate. Ask permission if you decide to publish a sample question or answer. Whatever your policy, make sure you inform your users what it is.

STEP 8: IMPLEMENT LIVE VIRTUAL REFERENCE

Implementing is the nitty-gritty of getting your service off the ground. It's important to finally leave the planning stage and to start actually answering live virtual reference questions. Many libraries call their first foray into live reference a "pilot project." Since live virtual reference is such a new way to provide service, the pilot project is a good way to learn by trial and error. View the project as a work in progress and be willing to make and learn from your mistakes. Many libraries that have implemented live reference spoke about being eager to just get some kind of service up to see what would happen. Some libraries literally just throw up a link on their Web pages and learn as they go along.

To keep implementation on track, have a timeline and work backwards from the date of your launch. Design the Web page or pages that will link to your service. Install the software and make sure it works from the librarian side and the user's side. Firm up the reference schedule and make sure everyone is trained. Customize the software to your specific situation by creating scripted responses if your software has that feature. If you are nervous about everything working correctly, explain to your users that you are operating a pilot project. Most will be understanding of minor glitches.

STEP 9: EVALUATE LIVE VIRTUAL REFERENCE

At the end of the pilot project period, or after your service has been operating for a set period of time, step back and take a look at what's working and what isn't. What are the problems and how can you fix them? How comfortable is the staff with answering questions? If you have a question log, analyze it. How well are questions getting answered? Are patrons actually getting their questions answered in real-time or are they being shunted to e-mail? Have there been users waiting on a hold queue? Are users satisfied with the service they are receiving? How many questions are coming in? What times are questions most frequent? How well is the software working? Is it working as you envisioned? If it is a pilot project, will you continue the service as is, make changes, or discontinue it altogether?

In our first pilot project at Temple, we discovered problems with our software. One of the worst problems was the limited time there was to respond to the audio cue. If a question came in and a librarian didn't respond in the initial 60 seconds the user was redirected to our e-mail reference form. This raised the expectation of real-time service but did not deliver. Even after the librarians responded initially, there were time limits on the exchange. This put librarians under additional unnecessary time pressure. Another problem was that our software did not display a running text of the conversation so it was difficult to keep track of the interaction. The librarian typed something in and sent it off and it was gone. So it was very easy to forget what you were talking about. Not good for librarians trying to get used to a new communications medium. These problems led us to look for new software and ultimately create our own, which led us back to the beginning of the planning process. For more on evaluation, see Chapter 10.

> **Checklist for Planning for Live Virtual Reference**
>
> - Articulate a Vision
> - Form a Committee
> - Gather Information
> - Investigate Funding
> - Decide on Staffing
> - Select Software
> - Draft Policy
> - Implement
> - Evaluate

SUMMARY

Planning for live virtual reference is an iterative as well as a sequential process. While you are gathering information you may alter your vision. The software that is currently available will affect how you staff your service. The amount of funding you have will affect what kind of software you will use. After your service has been up and running for a while, you may have to revisit or even begin certain aspects of the planning process over again. After you get a feel for what is working and what isn't, revisit earlier decisions you made: a change in software may necessitate tweaking your vision; a staffing model that isn't working may lead you to change your policy; new funding opportunities may open up new possibilities for software; your experience may lead you to an entirely new vision of what live virtual reference is for your library. You will become very familiar with some of the planning steps. Some are so important that they require entire chapters of their own. To these important parts of the planning process we now turn.

REFERENCES

American Library Association. 1995. *Code of Ethics of the American Library Association* [Online]. Available: www.ala.org/Alaorg/oif/ethics.html [2002, April 29].

Boyer, Joshua. 2001. "Virtual Reference at North Carolina State: The First One Hundred Days." *Information Technology and Libraries* 20: 122–128.

Pew Internet & American Life Project. 2000. *Trust and Privacy Online: Why Americans Want to Rewrite the Rules* (August) [Online]. Available: www.pewinternet.org/reports/toc.asp?Report=19 [2002, April 29].

Thibodeau, Patrick. 2002. "The Roots of Mistrust Go Deep." *Computerworld* 10 (March 4): 10.

5 GATHERING INFORMATION ON LIVE VIRTUAL REFERENCE

EXPLORE THE EXTERNAL ENVIRONMENT

When thrown into the unknown, it's natural, especially for librarians, to have the urge to gather information. Before initiating a project in your library, it's definitely a good idea to do your research and take a close look at what other libraries are doing and how they are doing it. Every successful library that we have talked to went through this phase. Doing so accomplishes a number of objectives.

For members of your planning committee or library who are skittish or skeptical about live virtual reference, identifying libraries that have actually implemented the service can give them confidence that your library can do it too. It can also give you ammunition that your library *needs* to be doing it. If libraries in your region are offering a new service but you aren't, how does that make your library look? In addition, by locating libraries that are offering live virtual reference in your area you sow the seeds for possible future collaboration.

By being familiar with and talking to librarians who have implemented live virtual reference, you will gain a first-hand knowledge of the different service models in use. It will be easier to find a model that fits your particular situation, and you can save time by copying or adapting what others have already done. You find out beforehand what mistakes they have made so you can sidestep them. Although sometimes belittled as "how we done it good" stories, looking at what other libraries are successfully doing is an important way that librarians learn from each other. Exploring other libraries deepens your understanding, gives you confidence, saves you time, and gives you new ideas. Soon you will be telling other librarians how you do it!

WEB PAGES

Fortunately, it's easy to find out which libraries are offering live virtual reference services, thanks to some industrious librarians. Two Web pages in particular are worth mentioning as starting points: Gerry McKiernan's *LiveRef(sm): A Registry of Real-time*

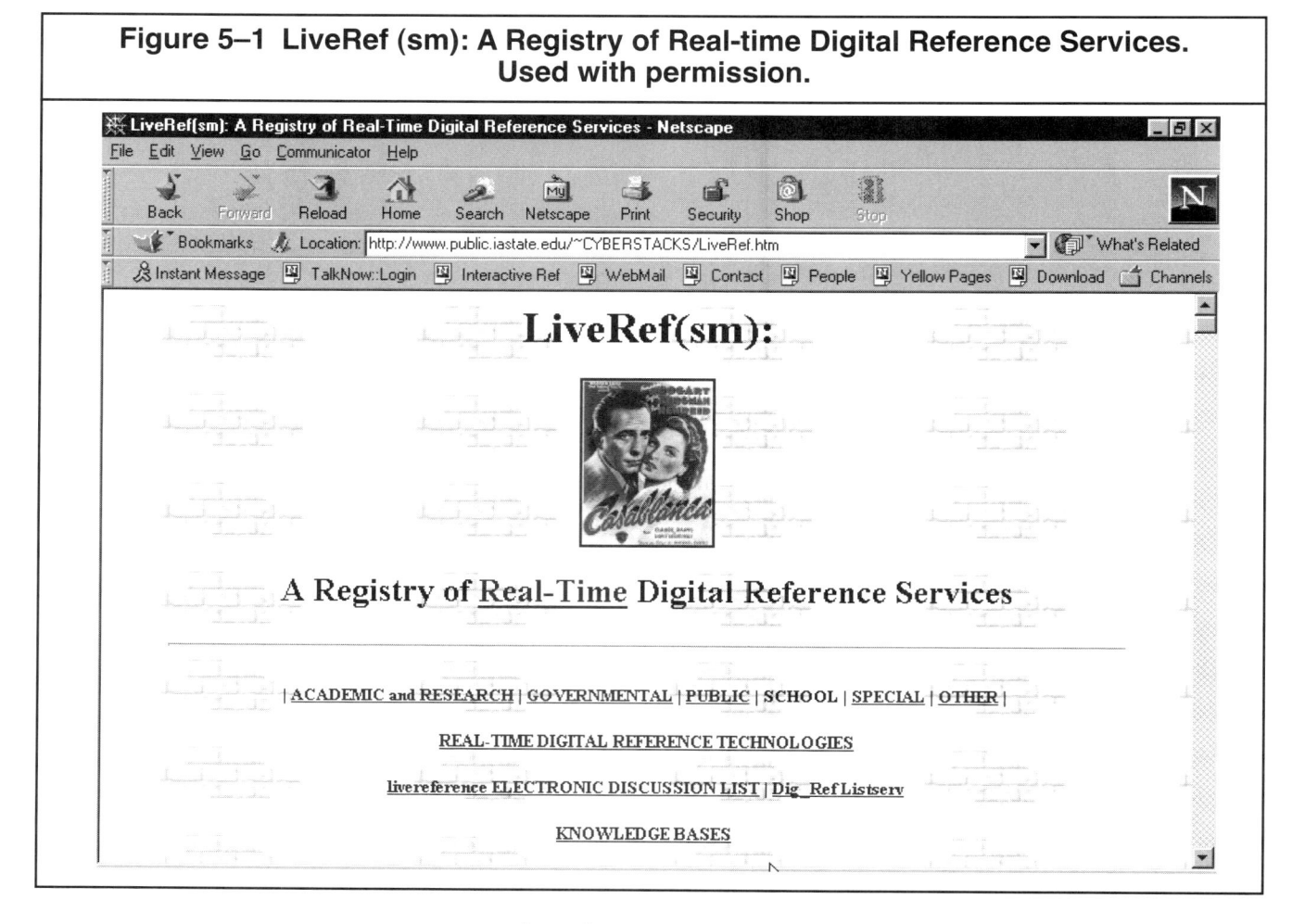

Figure 5–1 LiveRef (sm): A Registry of Real-time Digital Reference Services. Used with permission.

Digital Reference Services and Stephen Francoeur's *The Teaching Librarian.*

LiveRef(sm)—www.public.iastate.edu/~CYBERSTACKS/LiveRef.htm

On LiveRef(sm), librarian Gerry McKiernan of Iowa State University lists libraries that are offering live virtual reference services by type of library, including academic and research, governmental, public, school, special, and other. The Scout Report called LiveRef(sm) "a great resource for both users looking for an online reference librarian and librarians interested in instituting a Web-based, real-time reference service" (Scout Report, 2001). A quick scan of the list tells you the name of the library, the name of the service, and the name of the software the library is using. Hypertext links take you directly to that part of the library's Web page where users can connect in real-time. (In case you're wondering, the Casablanca photo on the home page is just a decoration.)

As of this writing, McKiernan's registry lists 116 libraries: 84 academic and research, three governmental, 14 public, one special, and 14 libraries included under "other." The number of public libraries on McKiernan's list may be underreported because libraries that are part of consortiums are not listed individually. McKiernan also provides a list of 26 kinds of software under the heading "Real-Time Reference Technologies." Although software won't be fully discussed until Chapter 7, get in the habit of looking at which software programs libraries are using. McKiernan also includes links to listservs, bibliographies, conferences, and surveys, making this page a one-stop-shop for links to information on live virtual reference.

The Teaching Librarian—pages.prodigy.net/tabo1/chatindex.htm

Next, move on to Stephen Francoeur's *Teaching Librarian* Web page (Figure 5–2). Francoeur, a librarian at Baruch College, devotes a section of his page to digital reference, which is further divided into e-mail, Web forms, chat reference, and Web contact centers. Francoeur explains clearly what the different types of digital reference services are and what the differences are between them. We are most interested in the section on chat reference because it has information on libraries offering live virtual reference as opposed to e-mail virtual reference services. The section on Web call centers is also of interest because it lists and describes software programs.

One of the most useful features of Francoeur's page is his index of chat reference services organized by consortium, country (and state within the United States), library type, and software. By examining these lists, you can get a clear picture of the different types of libraries, their geographical locations, the software they are using, and how they are collaborating with each other. For example, by examining the list of libraries sorted by "Consortia, Partnerships, Collaborations, and Informal Networks," you can find out which libraries are involved in collaborative projects. Francoeur also has a section on "Collaborative Networks" in which he discusses issues in starting a collaborative service and provides helpful links.

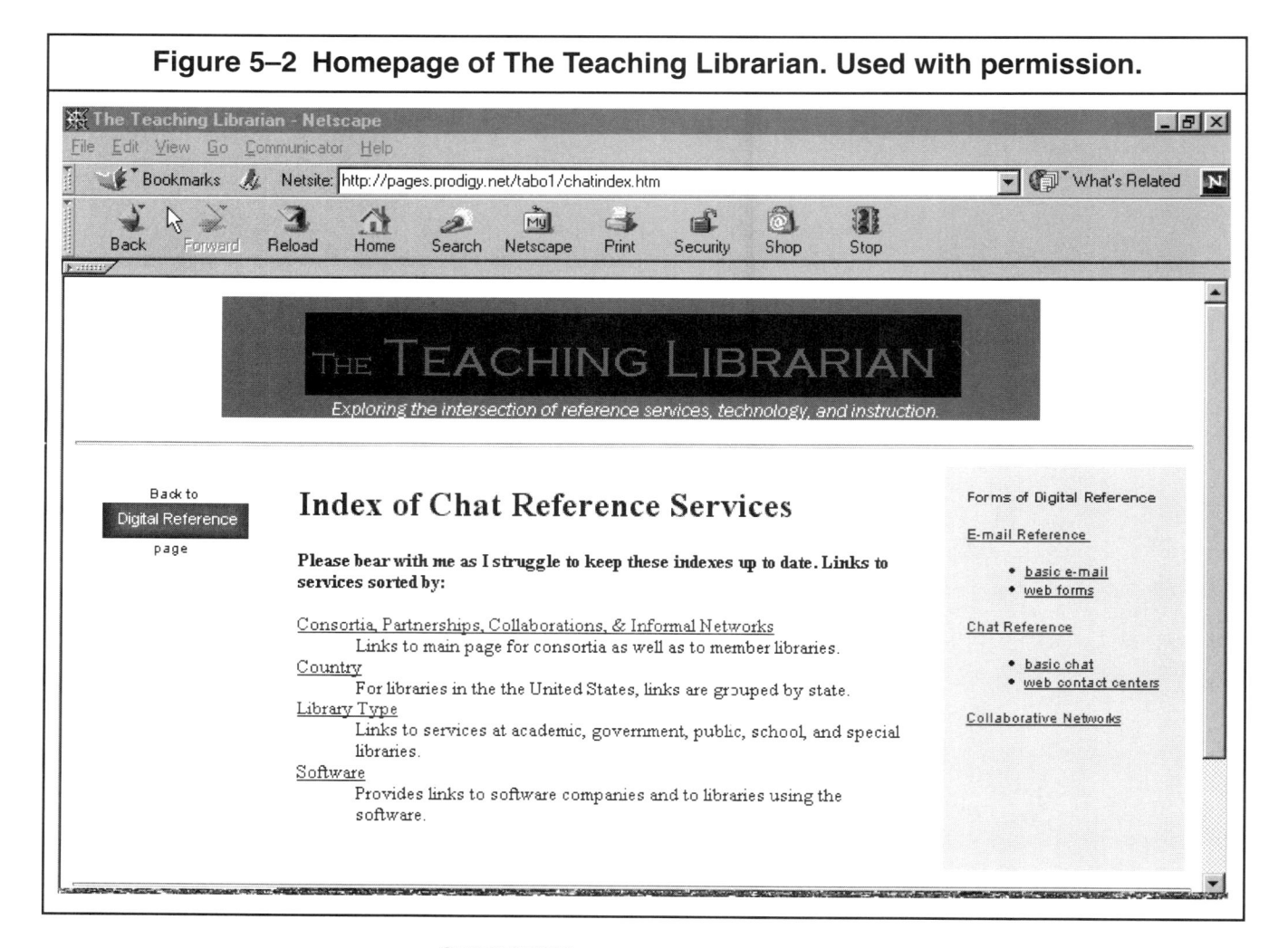

Figure 5-2 Homepage of The Teaching Librarian. Used with permission.

SURVEYS

Another way to gather information externally is to conduct a survey. Again, some of the difficult work has already been done for you. Matt Marsteller and Paul Neuhaus of Carnegie Mellon University Libraries developed a survey instrument and created a Web form (Figure 5-3) to solicit responses in the summer of 2001. To see the entire list of questions, visit www.contrib.andrew.cmu.edu/~matthewm/survey.html.

Marsteller and Neuhaus received 67 responses to their survey. Some of the interesting findings include:

- 97% of libraries reported using reference librarians to staff the service instead of paraprofessionals or students.
- 71% reported no increase in hours of reference services per week.

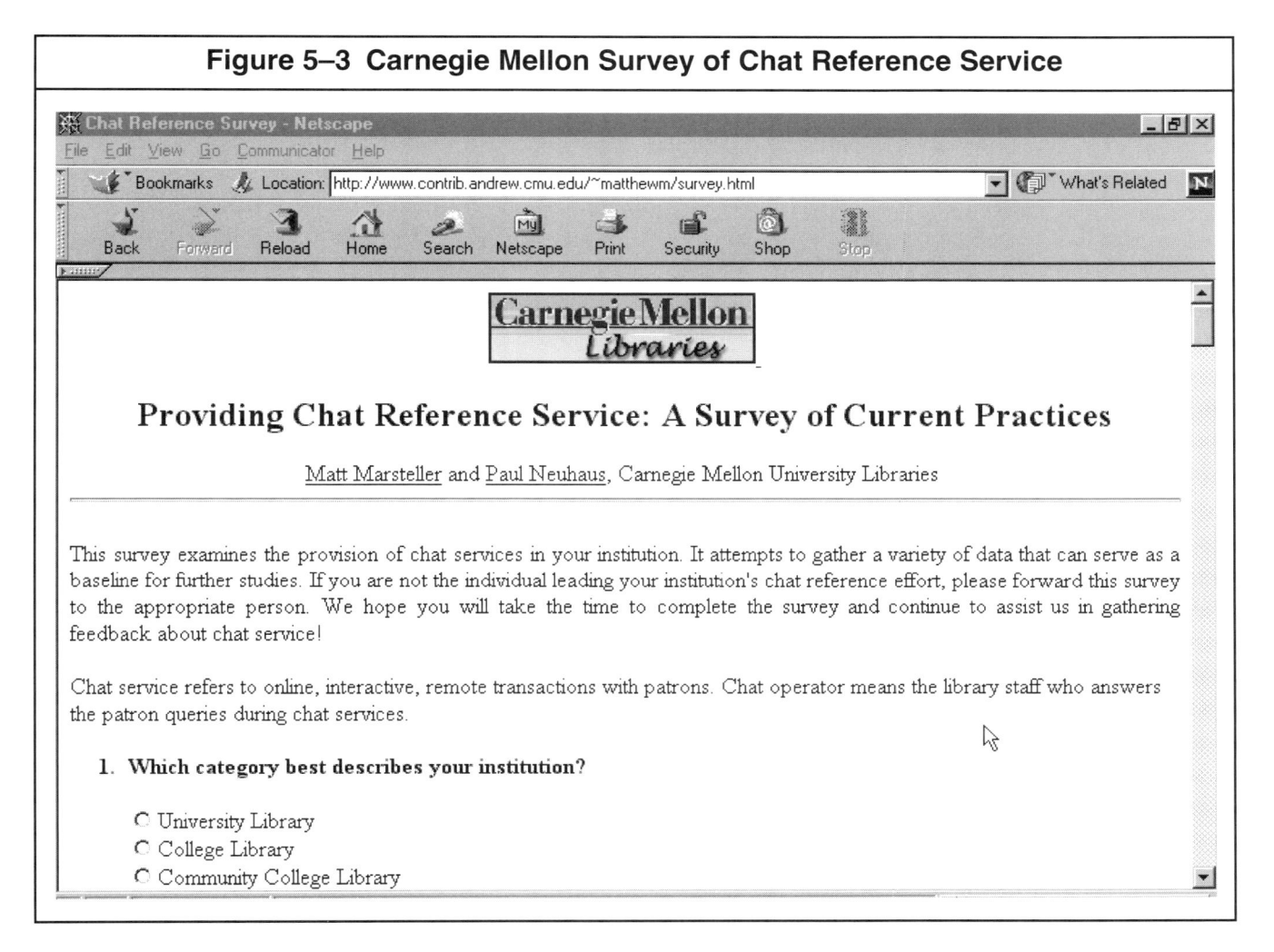

Figure 5–3 Carnegie Mellon Survey of Chat Reference Service

Providing Chat Reference Service: A Survey of Current Practices

Matt Marsteller and Paul Neuhaus, Carnegie Mellon University Libraries

This survey examines the provision of chat services in your institution. It attempts to gather a variety of data that can serve as a baseline for further studies. If you are not the individual leading your institution's chat reference effort, please forward this survey to the appropriate person. We hope you will take the time to complete the survey and continue to assist us in gathering feedback about chat service!

Chat service refers to online, interactive, remote transactions with patrons. Chat operator means the library staff who answers the patron queries during chat services.

1. Which category best describes your institution?

   ○ University Library
   ○ College Library
   ○ Community College Library

- 47% of respondents reported that the service was "definitely worth the money the institution spent on it, while 34% said it was "probably worth it."
- Most libraries reported service hours between 12 noon and 5:00 p.m.
- A majority of the libraries responding reported spending under $2,500 annually on the service, but 40% expected their service to change in the coming year.

Marsteller and Neuhaus presented the full results at the 2001 Virtual Reference Desk Conference in Orlando. The presentation is available at www.vrd.org/conferences/VRD2001/proceedings/neuhaus.shtml.

Conducting your own survey can be useful, especially if you are in a consortium and want to get a feel for what your members are doing or want to do. A survey need not be time consuming or complicated—it could be as simple as an informal poll. One consortium member told us that at one of the consortium's executive board meetings, a member simply asked "who would be interested in offering a live reference service?" Everyone's hand shot up and soon they were planning their service.

LISTSERVS

Not everyone has the time to design, conduct, and evaluate a good survey. Even if you did, it can be difficult to get enough respondents and the results can be difficult to interpret. In short, surveys are often just not feasible. Fortunately, there are two active listservs for discussions on live virtual reference: DIG_REF and livereference. If you have a question, a quick post to these listservs usually generates dozens of helpful replies. If you lurk long enough, eventually you'll see discussions of just about every aspect of live virtual reference. To subscribe to DIG_REF send an e-mail message to: LISTSERV@LISTSERV.SYR.EDU. In the first line of the message, type: SUBSCRIBE DIG_REF Firstname Lastname. To subscribe to livereference go to http://groups.yahoo.com/group/livereference.

DIG_REF is the broader of the two lists because it covers all aspects of digital reference, including e-mail virtual reference. The livereference listserv was created specifically for live virtual reference but gets less traffic than DIG_REF. Some recent postings on DIG_REF include virtual reference and distance learners, marketing virtual reference, announcements of new products, reports of usage statistics, and discussions of virtual reference standards.

TELEPHONE INTERVIEWS

Of course you can also always pick up the phone and talk to one of your colleagues involved in live virtual reference. At Temple we have spoken to a great number of libraries about our service. Common questions are: what kind of questions are you getting? How did you pick your software? What hours are you offering the service? Most librarians will be flattered you are interested and will be enthusiastic about talking about their new service to you. Software vendors are also a good source of information when you get to the stage of deciding on software.

BIBLIOGRAPHIES

The literature on live virtual reference is large and growing. Searching databases and the Web for articles can be frustrating due to the large number of terms in use to describe the concept. Again librarians have come to the rescue by creating bibliographies of books and articles. A good bibliography that's not too overwhelming can be found on Gerry McKiernan's LiveRef Web site, available at www.public.iastate.edu/~CYBERSTACKS/LiveRef.htm. For a more comprehensive treatment that includes all types of digital reference, see Bernie Sloan's *Digital Reference Services: A Bibliography* at http://alexia.lis.uiuc.edu/~b-sloan/digiref.html.

CONFERENCES

You've scoured the Web sites, looked at the formal surveys, lurked on the listservs, devoured the bibliographies, and still can't get enough? Time to hit the conferences to actually meet other live virtual reference fanatics like yourself in person. One of the most valuable aspects of conferences is the opportunity to talk to others who have been in the trenches. Published reports are usually summaries of projects with important particulars left out. Meeting face-to-face offers the chance to ask follow-up questions and to make a personal connection. You can get more details over lunch or chatting after a presentation about how a library coped with staffing problems or dealt with complications encountered with learning interactive communication techniques that no one anticipated.

How do you find conference sessions on live virtual reference? Start with the American Library Association's Annual Conference. You may even be able to attend an all day pre-conference on live virtual reference. If you can't make it to ALA Annual, sessions on live virtual reference are plentiful at local and regional conferences as well. Finding a program on digital reference is not as difficult as finding a seat—these sessions are usually packed. The granddaddy of all digital reference conferences is the Virtual Reference Desk Conference that has been held annually for the past three years. There you'll hear the most advanced practitioners discuss the latest trends in all aspects of digital reference services. For past proceedings and information on upcoming conferences visit their Web site at www.vrd.org/. For examples of other conferences and workshops see LiveRef(sm) www.public.iastate.edu/~CYBERSTACKS/LiveRef.htm#Conferences.

ASSESS THE INTERNAL ENVIRONMENT

Is your library ready for live virtual reference? After gaining an understanding of what others are doing, you then need to turn your gaze to the internal situation at your own institution to assess your readiness for live virtual reference and figure out what is the best model for your situation. The internal environment consists of three areas: the broader institutional or community framework, the library as a whole, and the reference department within your library. Conditions in all three areas can influence the kind of live virtual reference service you can offer or even whether you will be able to offer one at all.

CONSIDER YOUR INSTITUTIONAL OR COMMUNITY FRAMEWORK

Almost all libraries fit into broader frameworks. The academic library has its university or college, the public library has its town or city, the special library has its company or organization. Figure out how well live virtual reference meshes with the mission and goals of the broader institution or community of which your library is a part. If you are in an academic library, is distance learning impacting your institution? Are your users spread out geographically across a number of campuses? Are your students mainly commuters or mostly residential? How wired is your campus? Do you have computer labs that are remote from the library? How strong a commitment is there in general to technology? Can you collaborate with another group on campus to offer live help, such as admissions or student life? Are faculty teaching Web-based classes? Is there a computer science class on campus in which students are looking for projects? How much money or systems support can you obtain from your institution?

Public librarians need to ask themselves a similar set of questions for their town or region. How receptive will the board of trustees be to a live help service? Do you serve patrons across a number of geographically dispersed branches? Are the patrons in your community computer users? Do you have a large percentage of older patrons or do you serve mainly young adults? Can live help be offered as part of a homework help service? Can you obtain grant money from your region?

Although probably almost no library's broader institutional mission will prohibit live virtual reference service, it can influence the shape of such a service. If the fit with the broader mission is tenuous, a small-scale basic service might be best. For example, if your mission includes serving mainly older patrons who do not use Internet chat, you probably don't want to jump in with expensive software. On the other hand, if the fit with your mission is good, such as a mandate to serve distance learners, chances are better for you to offer a more advanced version of the service with more features and longer hours. Obviously, the better the fit the more likely you will be to get proper funding support.

Checklist for Considering Your Institutional or Community Framework

Academic
1. Is distance learning important?
2. Are users spread out geographically across a number of campuses?
3. Are students mainly commuters or mostly residential?
4. How wired is your campus?
5. Do you have computer labs that are remote from the library?
6. How strong a commitment is there to technology?
7. Can you collaborate with another group on campus?
8. Are faculty teaching Web-based classes?
9. Is there a computer science class in which students are looking for projects?
10. Can you obtain money or support from your institution?

Public
1. How receptive will the board of trustees be?
2. Do you serve patrons across geographically dispersed branches?
3. Do you have a large percentage of older patrons?
4. Do you have a large percentage of young adult patrons?
5. Can live virtual reference be offered as part of a homework help service?
6. Can you obtain grant money from your region?

EXAMINE YOUR LIBRARY ENVIRONMENT

At the library level, you must match any proposed live service to your library's mission, balance your new service against other new projects, gain support from the administration and technical librarians, and assess membership in consortiums. In terms of mission, does your library aspire to be a technological leader that eagerly embraces new trends, or is your library content to sit and wait while others work out the bugs? Is serving patrons digitally the way you want to serve patrons? Assuming a live service fits in with your mission, what other projects are going on right now in your library? Are you in the midst of implementing a new automation system and planning for a new building? If so, then perhaps live reference will be relegated to the back burner or maybe you should start small with the basic model instead of the advanced.

Will you have the necessary administrative support for your project? Without it, funding and staff support will be an uphill battle. Many librarians contend that administrative support is crucial to a project's success. Equally important is technical support. How overloaded is your systems staff? Do you even have a systems staff? Is there a person you can go to for help with installa-

> **Checklist for Examining Your Library Environment**
>
> 1. Does your library aspire to be a technological leader or does it prefer to watch others work out the bugs?
> 2. What other projects are going on right now in your library?
> 3. Will you have administrative support?
> 4. Will you have technical support?
> 5. How overloaded is your systems staff?
> 6. Does your library have any technolgical constraints that limit chat?
> 7. Does your library belong to any consortiums?

tion, troubleshooting, maintenance, and the thousand and one other minor and major technical headaches that may occur as a result of your live virtual reference service? Will that person have time to help or will they be swamped with other duties? Maybe you have a whole team of techies sitting around with a lot of free time looking for new projects to work on. The University of Florida, for example, knew they could count on their excellent systems staff to install and maintain expensive software on their servers. This influenced their choice of software. Or perhaps your lack of systems staff necessitates that you purchase a package that requires no work on your end. Does your library have any technological constraints that you must work in, such as, "we don't allow any chat services on any of our servers?" How about consortiums? Is your library in any consortiums? If so, are they operating or planning to operate a live virtual reference service that you can participate in?

CONSIDER YOUR REFERENCE DEPARTMENT

Finally, you need to take stock of your current reference services. First and most importantly, are you currently offering a formal e-mail reference service? By formal we mean not just having a few reference librarians' e-mail addresses buried somewhere on your site who respond willy-nilly whenever someone sends in a question. We mean an actual link prominently placed on your home page called "Ask A Librarian" (or some similar name), and a formal procedure in place for answering questions. An established e-mail reference service is the foundation for live virtual reference. By participating in e-mail reference, your librarians will already have a familiarity with the basic principles and techniques of answering reference questions in a non face-to-face environment. Second, e-mail reference will serve as a fallback service for your live virtual reference service. When your live service is closed or unavailable, you should be able to allow your patron to submit their question by e-mail. If you don't currently offer a formal e-mail reference service, your first step is to start one.

For example, when the authors began their work together at Temple University, the Temple University Libraries were already offering e-mail reference service. Live virtual reference was the next logical step. When one of the authors (Marc Meola) left Temple to begin work at The College of New Jersey (TCNJ), however, he discovered no formalized e-mail reference service in place. To jump to a live service without an e-mail service would be premature. The first step to live virtual reference was the establishment of formal e-mail virtual reference service that included a link from the home page, a service policy, and a staffing model. If you are not currently offering e-mail virtual reference, initiate an e-mail virtual reference service before you begin to offer live virtual reference.

Next in order of importance are the characteristics of your reference librarians. Are they resistant to change or do they embrace it? Are they comfortable with multitasking? How do they handle pressure? Is your current in-house, physical reference desk service hectic or quiet? If there are slow periods, it may be possible to add a live virtual reference component to the duties of the reference librarians. If your desk receives a steady stream of patrons, however, simultaneous staffing of a physical and virtual desk will be a disservice to both physical and virtual patrons and a cause of vexation to your librarians. Many libraries report having some librarians who are enthusiastic about live digital services, some who are willing to go along with it, and some librarians who are outright hostile or strongly opposed to it. If you have too many in the latter camp, it will be difficult to implement a successful service. Also consider how your librarians will feel about having their answers evaluated, and who will do the evaluation. Be sure to get on the same page with your head of reference, if you have someone in that position. The head of reference needs to support the project and may need to take on new responsibilities relating to evaluating answers or assessing statistics.

> **Checklist for Considering Your Reference Department**
>
> 1. Do you currently offer a formal e-mail virtual reference service?
> 2. Are your librarians resistant to change or do they embrace it?
> 3. Are your librarians comfortable multitasking?
> 4. Is your desk service hectic or quiet?
> 5. How many librarians are opposed to live virtual reference?
> 6. Is your Head of Reference on board with the project?

SUMMARY

Gathering information about live virtual reference allays fears, saves time, and generates ideas for how to set up your service. Gather information on the external environment—what other libraries are doing—and the internal environment—what your library is doing. To find out what other libraries are doing, visit Web sites, conduct a survey, post or lurk on a listserv, talk to colleagues by telephone, read articles and reports from bibliographies, and attend conferences. To ensure that you aren't overwhelmed by all this information, filter it through your own internal situation. Assess your broader institutional or community setting, your own library's mission and existing services, and your own reference department. Having a handle on what other libraries are doing and how it relates to your library is a crucial precondition for the next two steps in planning a live virtual reference service: deciding on staffing and deciding on software.

REFERENCES

Scout Report. 2001. [Online]. Available http://scout.cs.wisc.edu/report/sr/2001/scout-010713.html#15. July 13, 2001.

6 DECIDING ON A STAFFING MODEL FOR LIVE VIRTUAL REFERENCE

As stated in Chapter 2, one of the obstacles to overcome in offering live virtual reference is coping with additional workload. Besides the additional work of planning, training, marketing, and evaluating a live virtual reference service, of pressing concern is deciding on a staffing model for how live virtual reference questions will be answered. After all, since live virtual reference is human help, you will have to provide real live human beings to answer questions. Ideally, these real live human beings will also be real live reference librarians, who will answer live virtual reference questions with the same education, training, and expertise that traditional in-person questions have always received. Once you arrive at a workable staffing model for answering live virtual reference questions at your library, you are more than halfway there in terms of being able to implement live virtual reference.

To decide on a staffing model, ask three questions:

- Who will answer questions?
- Where will questions be answered?
- When will questions be answered?

The answers to these questions can be viewed through the five models of live virtual reference, giving us five models of live virtual reference staffing: the basic staffing model, the homegrown staffing model, the advanced staffing model, the collaborative staffing model, and the corporate staffing model.

CHOOSE THE BASIC STAFFING MODEL

Since most of us are familiar and confident with the workings of the physical reference desk, the existing staffing and organization of the physical desk can easily serve as a foundation to build your live service. In fact, the simplest model for staffing can be a virtual replica of your physical reference desk. Who will answer live virtual questions? The same people who answer questions at your physical reference desk. Where will these live virtual questions be answered? At the physical reference desk. When will they be answered? The same hours the physical reference desk is open. Assuming the physical reference desk is not going away, this model simply adds the new live virtual service point on top of the in-person service. Real-time questions are answered at the desk along with in-person questions.

ADVANTAGES OF BASIC STAFFING MODEL

The advantage of this model is its simplicity and continuity. Simplicity means less work, continuity means less change, less change means less fear, less fear means less stress. Since the same librarians answer questions at the desk, no decisions have to be made about who will answer live virtual reference questions and who will not. All librarians who answer questions on the physical desk will answer questions on the live virtual desk.

Keep the hours of the live virtual service the same as in-person service: neither increase hours to 24/7, nor decrease to a complicated arrangement such as 1:00 p.m. to 5:00 p.m. on alternating Tuesdays and Thursdays. Increased hours would require more staff (which you don't have). Decreased or altered hours result in confusion for patrons. This service is to serve the patron's needs, after all. Patrons just want to have their questions answered, not worry about what time a service is operating. Decreased hours also decreases the amount of time your service is actually "live." If a patron has a question at 10:30 a.m., but your live service doesn't open until 1:00, then they have to wait two and a half hours to have their question answered. That's not service in real-time. The more your service hours are limited, the less "live" your service really is.

In the basic model, questions are answered by your librarians at the physical reference desk, not in offices, not from other libraries, not from librarian homes. This means no additional reference hours, no worrying about the quality of other librarians' (e.g. librarians from other libraries) answers to your patron's questions, and no worrying about comp time or union work rules for librarians working from home. The major advantage to the model is that it minimizes the amount of workload that is added to the library. Since it is simple, it requires less planning than other models. The riddle of how to add service without increasing staff is solved.

DISADVANTAGES OF BASIC STAFFING MODEL

But is it? Perhaps, but at a price. The main disadvantage of this model is that answering simultaneous in-person queries and live digital queries at the same location has proven to be difficult and stressful for librarians. Add the telephone to the mix and your reference librarians will feel like they are juggling a chain saw, a bowling ball, and a flaming torch. A consensus is forming among librarians offering live virtual reference that working with an in-person patron and a live virtual reference patron simultaneously is close to impossible. You can't give your full attention to either patron and as a result service to both suffers.

This topic came up recently on the digital reference listserv DIGREF. Paul Nehaus, a librarian at Carnegie Mellon University, said, "the couple of times I covered chat at the reference desk and had simultaneous chat and in-person questions, I did not think I did a very thorough job of serving either patron" (Nehaus, 2001). When multiple questions come in at once or when one query becomes too complex, Kelly Broughton of Bowling Green State University added that "something has to give, usually it's not the in-person patron" (Broughton, 2001).

One strategy to adopt when you get simultaneous chat and in-person questions is to ask one of the patrons to wait while you help the other one. You can ask the virtual patron to wait, but unfortunately, most of the time they don't want to wait. As a result they often just abandon their call. If they do agree to wait, sometimes librarians will (unintentionally, of course) forget they are still there after dealing with the in-person patron.

In-person patrons have even more difficulty waiting. They find it difficult to understand that you are online with another patron just like them. Their attitude is "Hey, I'm standing here in front of you, help me now!" Since the virtual patron is invisible to the person waiting at the desk, the in-person patron cannot see that you are helping someone. Traditionally, many librarians feel that in-person patrons should receive priority over telephone or digital patrons. These librarians seem to think that if someone actually gets up the energy to bring their physical body into the library, then they should be rewarded. Yet this speaks against one of our core values—service equity. Although old habits die hard, many librarians are coming to believe that the remote or live digital patron deserves the same level of service as the in-person patron.

Another disadvantage of answering live digital transactions at the physical reference desk is that the inherent time pressure of live reference is intensified. In live virtual reference, there is pressure on the librarian to formulate responses rapidly and articulate answers concisely. At a busy reference desk, with in-person patrons waiting, this pressure is heightened. As a result, librarians may try to compensate by rushing their answers or by giving incomplete answers. Inaccurate answers are often a consequence.

Basic Staffing Model
• Virtual replica of physical reference desk • Virtual questions answered at the physical desk • Virtual hours same as physical hours • Advantages—simplicity, continuity • Disadvantages—juggling in-person with virtual queries problematic, service to both suffers

In general, librarians cannot give a query the full attention it deserves. Hardly the impression we want to make when we encourage people to choose us over the Internet. For these reasons, only libraries that receive very limited desk traffic can attempt to combine live virtual reference with face-to-face in-person reference. More and more libraries that offer live virtual reference are abandoning the basic staffing model and in its place turning to a more complex model.

IMPLEMENT THE HOMEGROWN STAFFING MODEL

With the homegrown model, you are not tied into any specific staffing arrangement in terms of answering questions, since the only difference between the homegrown model and the other models is the software. A homegrown model can accommodate a basic staffing model, or an advanced staffing model. The only thing different about the homegrown model is that you need staff who are either capable enough to download open source software, proficient enough to modify existing code, or expert enough to create it from scratch with your specifications.

Homegrown Staffing Model
• Can accommodate basic or advanced arrangement • Depends on having technical staff to download and modify software

ADOPT THE ADVANCED STAFFING MODEL

The advanced model solves the problem of the stressful and ineffective simultaneous reference transaction by uncoupling live digital question answering from in-person traditional desk question answering. In the advanced model, live virtual reference questions are answered somewhere away from the traditional reference desk. Usually this means librarians answer questions in their offices, at a new desk devoted solely to live virtual reference, or sometimes even at home. Since the number of live questions received tends to be few, especially in the beginning, the library may decide to pull their phone and e-mail reference services off their traditional desks as well and combine them with live virtual reference. This is the staffing model that has been adopted by North Carolina State University (Boyer, 2001). Even if call volume grows, the combination of phone, e-mail, and chat questions are more suited to juggling than the in-person query. This staffing arrangement allows librarians to give fuller attention to e-mail and live reference questions, while freeing librarians at the physical desk to concentrate on in-person patrons.

PROBLEMS WITH THE ADVANCED STAFFING MODEL AND THEIR SOLUTIONS

Although this staffing arrangement solves one problem, it creates others. When live virtual reference question answering is disjoined from the physical reference desk, a second reference schedule must be created and maintained. This means more reference hours for reference librarians in addition to their already existing physical desk hours. Reference librarians will have less time to spend on activities such as library instruction, committee work, collection development, liaison, community outreach, story time, or special events planning. Of course more administrative time will also be needed to create the second schedule and make sure people are following it.

This is a vexing problem for the advanced staffing model. One way to get around it is to transfer staff from the physical reference desk to the virtual reference desk. For example, if you have two reference librarians at a physical reference desk, take one off the physical desk and put him or her on the virtual reference desk. Of course this depends on having more than one librarian staffing the physical desk, and it also depends on traffic at the physical desk being not as high as it once was.

HOURS OF THE ADVANCED STAFFING MODEL

Other libraries have limited the number of hours the live virtual reference desk is staffed. At Cornell University, for example, live virtual reference is available from 1:00 p.m. to 5:00 p.m., reducing the number of hours that librarians are required to staff it. If these hours can be spread out over a large number of librarians, then their additional desk time may be minimal—one to two extra hours per week. Other libraries have limited hours and hired additional staff. The Van Pelt Library at the University of Pennsylvania has provided live virtual reference from 9:00 p.m. to 2:00 a.m. and at least initially hired a designated librarian to staff this service point specifically.

This is another characteristic of the advanced model: the hours are often not the same as the physical reference desk. Limited hours are okay for a trial, but librarians are finding that they don't receive enough questions during limited hours, especially if the hours are during the day. More and more libraries are looking at expanded hours—hours that extend later into the evening or even 24/7 hours. This further complicates staffing. Not only will librarians have to work additional hours, they will have to work hours during which they are normally accustomed to sleeping. Some libraries have solved this problem by outsourcing late evening and early morning hours to librarians provided by software vendors.

WHO ANSWERS QUESTIONS IN THE ADVANCED STAFFING MODEL

Who answers live virtual reference questions in the advanced model? Since questions are separated from the physical reference desk, the librarians who do serve at the desk need not specifically be required to answer live virtual reference questions. This raises the possibility of having the live virtual reference service staffed only by librarians who volunteer (willingly) to participate. This can be one way to solve the problem of staff opposition to live virtual reference, and can also be a way to make better use of staff members whose temperament and inclination is more suited to live virtual reference. On the other hand, by letting some staff members opt out, those staff members will not have the skills that other librarians are acquiring. It can also lead to further tension as some begin to view the workload distribution as inequitable.

When live virtual reference staffing is separated from physical reference staffing, new possibilities and questions arise. Should you involve branch librarians? If so, will they need to be trained to answer new and different questions? What about paraprofessionals? One librarian admitted that while paraprofessionals are permitted to staff their chat reference service, they always make sure a professional librarian is available for in-person queries. Again, this is a question of service equity. Why doesn't the chat patron deserve service from a professional as well?

WHERE ARE QUESTIONS ANSWERED IN THE ADVANCED STAFFING MODEL

Where will questions be answered in the advanced model? As was mentioned earlier, live virtual reference may be staffed by librarians in their homes. At first blush, it may sound great to be able to answer reference questions in your bunny slippers. Yet working from home is not without its complications. Do your librarians have the necessary computer hardware? Is their connection to the Internet fast enough? Does the Internet connection have to be paid for? Who will pay for it? Are there any union work rules about working from home? If a librarian gets hurt answering a question from home, are they eligible for compensation? Will they get compensatory time for these additional hours?

Another area of concern when librarians are moved away from a physical desk is that they lose access to important print reference materials. Many virtual reference librarians poo-poo this problem. They say that the overwhelming majority of reference questions can now be answered with online sources instead of print reference materials. Still, we all know how useful it is to have a few trusty print reference books close by in a pinch: the *Statistical Abstract of the United States*, an almanac, a good dictionary or encyclopedia, and various others depending on your library and the type of questions you receive. One should also keep in mind that some local questions require a phone book, a desk rolodex, or some other local crib sheet.

It is true that there are extensive reference resources available on the Web. A well-organized collection of reference Web sites such as the ones at the Internet Public Library or the Librarian's Index to the Internet is an important component of your ability to provide reference service, in-person or live digital, but live virtual reference especially. Some libraries even put a link to collections like this on the Web page where the user submits the question. But again the question of answer quality and service equity arises. Be careful not to push a Web source on a digital patron simply because it is on the Web if it is not the best source for the question. If patrons can be pushed to some Web site or other that is somehow related to the query, but a better print reference book could answer the question more authoritatively, you may be compromising your standards. In designing the live virtual reference

> **Advanced Staffing Model**
>
> - Separate virtual reference desk from physical reference desk
> - Can be staffed by volunteers only
> - Librarians may answer questions from home
> - Advantages—Allows librarians to give undivided attention to patrons
> - Disadvantages—Complicates reference scheduling, more reference hours for librarians

desk, we recommend that, as much as possible, live virtual reference librarians should have access to all the materials that will contribute toward answering a question with as much speed and accuracy as possible.

The advanced staffing model in which librarians answer live virtual reference questions away from the physical reference desk does solve the problem of librarians having to answer live digital queries at the same time as in-person queries. But the advanced model also has its own problems. A second reference schedule must be created and reference librarians will have to spend more time answering reference questions instead of pursuing other activities. The hours of the live digital service may be shorter or longer than those of the physical reference desk. If hours are extended, this will mean even more work for the reference librarians. If hours are limited, patrons may be confused and will not submit enough questions. Working away from the desk separates the librarian from print resources, which may affect answer quality. If questions are answered from home, the library may be opening itself to new liabilities. Are these problems surmountable? Some libraries hope to avoid these problems with the collaborative model.

PARTICIPATE IN THE COLLABORATIVE STAFFING MODEL

As we have seen, one of the main problems with the advanced model is that it is more work for the library, particularly the reference librarians who answer the questions. To solve this problem, some libraries are using their memberships in consortia to

Collaborative Staffing Model
• Use membership in consortia to share staffing • Advantages—Workload is distributed, reduces burden on individual librarians • Disadvantages—Requires more training, coordination, administration

share the burden of staffing live virtual reference services. Here's how it works: since live virtual reference software allows librarians to answer questions from any place that has a Web connection, librarians do not have to be in one central location to answer questions. Librarians from anywhere in a state or region then can log on as an "operator" and staff a live virtual reference service. The more librarians that are available, the fewer the hours any one librarian has to contribute. Instead of having to provide 80 hours a week of live virtual reference, any one particular library in a consortium may only have to provide 4–6 hours a week. The workload is distributed among all the consortium members. You have a much larger pool of librarians available. It reduces the burden on individual libraries and librarians so that any one librarian may only have to devote a few extra hours of reference a week. While the concern is usually how to keep the number of hours down for any one person, there is a minimum amount of live virtual reference time required for librarians to become proficient and maintain their virtual proficiency. One needs at least a few hours a week to stay sharp. Many of these libraries have volunteers who willingly and enthusiastically come forward to be a part of the new high-profile project.

The disadvantages of the collaborative model are that it requires more training, more administering, and closer monitoring for quality answers. Librarians require more training because not only must they be aware of the policies and frequently asked questions from their own library, but they must learn the policies and questions of other libraries as well. If the collaborative service has its own policies, all the member libraries must agree on what they are. Collaborative models often have at least one full-time person who administers the project, including the extensive scheduling that is required. This person may also monitor the answers for some standard of quality, so that question answers are somewhat uniform across the service.

BEWARE OF THE CORPORATE STAFFING MODEL

Wouldn't it be odd to walk into a store, ask for help, and be told to wait because the salesperson was working with an online customer? Perhaps this should be a message to librarians not to mix live virtual reference with live face-to-face reference. Corporate call centers are usually located away from in-person areas, and depending on call volume, operators may work in large rooms filled with cubicles. Outsourcing of this function is common, and call operators may be dispersed throughout the country or even in foreign countries. Corporate customer service agents may have to spend all day, every day providing customer service. Some corporate call centers handle thousands of calls per hour. Compensation for employees working in these positions is not the greatest—this combined with the work conditions make staff turnover one of the biggest challenges that corporate call centers face.

Many corporate call centers that experience high volume use a sophisticated algorithm called Erlang C to determine how many operators are needed to answer questions at any one time. Erlang C was originally developed to apply to telephone calls, but it can be applied to Web-based question answering services as well (for an example of an Erlang C calculator see www.prefsolutions.com/html/calc.htm). Library Systems and Services (LSSI) actually uses Erlang C to calculate the staffing requirements of their virtual reference center. For more detail on how to apply Erlang C to libraries, see Coffman and Saxton's 1999 article, "Staffing the Reference Desk in the Largely Digital Library."

Many librarians are, perhaps with good reason, wary of corporate model staffing scenarios being played out in libraries. Modeling a librarian position on a customer call center employee would be a step backward for most librarians. Dismantling the physical reference desk or staffing it with paraprofessionals and routing questions to librarians who are constantly on call makes many librarians nervous. Most librarians have other duties besides providing reference service, and to increase reference hours would mean that these other duties would be not be attended to. It would also mean librarians would be more susceptible to burnout and libraries would face problems with staff turnover. Although the corporate model has some good lessons for the library, perhaps the staffing arrangement is more of a cautionary tale than a model to be replicated.

Corporate Call Center Staffing Model
• Staff located away from in-person areas • Low pay and high turnover • Uses Erlang C to calculate staffing requirements • Cautionary tale for librarians?

SUMMARY

Deciding on a staffing model is one of the most important decisions in planning a live virtual reference service. There is no one model that is right for every library, but some models fit some libraries better than others. A reference desk with moderate to low traffic can do very well with the basic staffing model. On the other hand, the advanced staffing model—pulling staff off the physical reference desk and creating a separate virtual reference desk—is a great idea if you have the staff and the question volume to support it. As of this writing, most academic libraries are using either the basic staffing model or the advanced staffing model. Public libraries, however, are using the collaborative model to great advantage. The corporate model is even influencing libraries, giving us new ways of calculating staffing needs. Choose the staffing model that fits your library best. Only one other planning issue will affect your live virtual reference service more, and that is selecting software.

REFERENCES

Boyer, Joshua. 2001. "Virtual Reference at North Carolina State: The First One Hundred Days." *Information Technology and Libraries* 20 (September): 122–128.

Broughton, Kelly. DIG_REF 11/1/01. Accessed 4/29/02.

Coffman, Steve, and Matthew L. Saxton. 1999. "Staffing the Reference Desk in the Largely-Digital Library." *The Reference Librarian* 66: 141–163.

Neuhaus, Paul. DIG_REF 11/1/01. Accessed 4/29/02.

7 SELECTING SOFTWARE FOR LIVE VIRTUAL REFERENCE— FIVE OPTIONS

Although you may only be familiar with a few live virtual reference software programs, there are currently over 20 different packages in use in libraries (Francouer, 2001) and over 50 programs available on the market (Coffman, 2001). New programs and companies are springing into existence every day, while at the same time companies and their programs are disappearing into dot-com oblivion. The cost of live virtual reference software can range from free to into the tens of thousands of dollars. To add further nuance to the picture, many vendors offer different levels of their product from basic to more sophisticated with more features and a higher price tag.

It's up to you and your planning committee to sort through this mess. Selecting software means taking an inventory of what software programs are available, what the features are, how much they cost, and how well they fit your institution. In this chapter, we'll guide you through these decisions by showing you how to:

- Put software in perspective
- Involve your systems staff
- Ask the right questions

Then we'll take a more detailed look at some of the major software programs and group them into our familiar five categories: basic, homegrown, advanced, collaborative, and corporate. It's true that software is "always changing" and information about software goes out of date almost as soon as it's written down, but you have to start somewhere.

PUT SOFTWARE IN PERSPECTIVE

There can be a tendency to focus almost exclusively on the software and make this the focal point of your efforts when developing a service. Don't get too hung up on the software and let that drive the whole decision-making process. As we've discussed, you need to take a look at your unique situation with its particular idiosyncrasies. The software you select can and probably will change along the way. New features will be added to a package or you may choose to switch to a different package. There are a number of examples of libraries that have been doing live virtual reference for two or three years and have experimented with two or more programs. They tried one that didn't meet all their needs and moved on to another system. The MCLS consortium in California, for example, actually switched software partway through the initial implementation of their service. Originally they chose Webline software (the software that Lands' End uses) but then migrated to a version of the eGain software (the software modified by 24/7 and LSSI). One thing you can count on is that the technology will change and probably change faster than we can keep up with. But keep in mind that you're providing human help and the technology is there to assist and facilitate that process.

Two common patterns have emerged related to choosing software. The first is for a library to decide to do live reference and choose a free or inexpensive software package, just to get going. Then either they are satisfied with the basic software, or they move on to a more advanced (and more expensive) service once they discover some of the shortcomings of the basic software.

The second pattern involves library consortiums that begin with the more advanced software programs. The consortial arrangement allows them to spread the cost and the workload among many libraries. The funding for the consortiums has usually come from grants. Choosing one of the more full featured systems means that you can easily invest thousands of dollars. This kind of investment provides a strong incentive to make the system work and to accept the challenges of a longer learning curve, various software glitches, and more time spent planning, coordinating, and evaluating. The group your library falls into will depend upon whether or not you belong to a consortium, how much funding is available for the project and how much interest and enthusiasm there is in your library for live virtual reference.

If you have the funding and the staff, a more advanced product can be very attractive. The page pushing and co-browsing features in particular, which give you the ability to show the patron Web sites and demonstrate how to search because your screens are in sync, are so powerful and add so much to the effectiveness of the transaction that it moves you to another level of service altogether. They personalize the interaction and give the user a real incentive to come back to you again.

Another important variable to consider is the user group for which the software was designed. Was it designed to help customer service representatives give you advice about buying a shirt for Uncle Harry? Or was it designed to allow librarians to provide guidance to their patrons?

The Voice over IP (VoIP) functionality, which would allow the librarian and patron to speak to each other while online, is a feature that holds tremendous promise. It has the potential to exponentially improve the quality of the transaction, but it's just not-quite-ready-for-prime-time yet. It is now included with some of the software packages on the market however, and it has shown us what's possible. We can envision a user sitting at home watching a librarian do a search on the Web and speaking to the librarian to ask questions and being given instructions during the process. Wouldn't you want to use a service like that?

INVOLVE YOUR SYSTEMS STAFF

Involve your systems staff as much as possible during the whole process of researching, selecting, and implementing a service. While this will often happen in the natural course of events, you need to make sure your technical staff are apprised of progress, demonstrations, and meetings along the way, so that they have an opportunity to provide input. They may be able to alert you to potential pitfalls and challenges of which you'd be otherwise unaware.

An example of the pitfalls of not involving your systems staff can be seen in this example of the implementation of a live reference service at a major university. An applications service provider (ASP) was chosen to host the live reference service, which meant that all transactions would be routed through the company's server. This arrangement is beneficial because it reduces demands on staff time and library hardware and software. Plans were made to launch the service at two branch locations. More librarians became aware of the project, really liked the idea and decided to expand the pilot project to the main campus. They neglected, however, to consult with the network administration group. Had they done so, they would have discovered that different computer operating systems were being used at different locations. So the live reference software worked fine at some places, but not at others.

The lesson here is that even though an ASP is hosting your

Checklist

1. Cost. Is it within your budget? Do you have a budget for this project? The open source software camp has solved this one by eliminating the need to purchase or subscribe. Other libraries have written grants to procure the necessary funds. Some lucky libraries have internal funds that can be designated or reallocated for this purpose. LSTA funds have been used by a number of libraries to finance projects. Also don't forget that the vendors can be very helpful in this regard. Their mission is to persuade the decision makers to purchase their product.

2. Does it require the user to download or install special software (client/plug-in) ? Having to download or install software is a barrier that you want to avoid if possible. This will be enough of an obstacle to prevent many people from trying the service.

3. Short or long learning curve? Do you need to make it as easy as possible for both staff and users? Or can you afford to set up a service that will be sufficiently attractive to both sides that they're willing to invest more time in learning how to use it?

4. Level of library systems support required. Do you have a large systems staff or none? Software capabilities have to match your situation.

5. Are users queued? Do they know it? The answers to both these questions should be yes. It should be possible for the librarian to see if someone just logged on and the user should know that someone has been alerted and will be able to help them, so they're not left hanging.

6. Does the package provide (or allow for) a Web-based online asynchronous reference service (e-mail) as backup? You want to make sure that an e-mail reference service is still an option for times when live reference isn't available.

7. Can more than one librarian log on simultaneously? You'll need this to be able to refer questions and to be able to handle multiple users if the service becomes popular. Also useful for monitoring the system.

8. Can a user be transferred? This would be important for instance in referring a user to a subject specialist or another librarian who's available.

9. What sort of archiving capability is available? You want to be able to maintain logs that are easily accessible and can be manipulated easily.

10. What kind of reports can be generated? You're going to want to gather statistical information and produce reports. Ask about the options available. Can you customize the reports?

11. Audio features. Being able to speak to the user can significantly enhance the quality of the interaction. Voice over IP (VoIP) is available with some products, but in many cases it may introduce as many problems as it solves.

Checklist (continued)

12. Co-browsing supported? This very powerful feature allows you to actually show the user where to go and how to get there because your browsers are in sync. Each screen that appears on your browser also appears simultaneously on the user's browser. This is expensive, but should be at the top of your list if you can afford it.

13. How secure are transactions? This is not as paramount as when you're sending your credit card number over the Net, but you want to know that your conversation is private.

14. Privacy. This refers not just to how private your conversation with a librarian is while it is happening (point of service), but also to how logs are maintained and whether the information is made available to others in the library, the larger organization, or third parties.

15. Do you have access to all the files? Can you review, download, and manipulate all the material in the archives whenever you like?

16. Interface—Can you modify it? You want to be able to use your own graphics if you choose and create a look and feel consistent with your vision of how you want your library to be presented to the world.

17. Icon/help button—Can it be modified? Can it be on any page? You should be able to use your own graphics if you wish and you want to be able to have buttons/links on as many pages as possible.

18. Vendor's reputation Talk to other librarians who are using a product. Are they satisfied with the service? Can they work with the vendor and how responsive is the company to library concerns? Are they focused on multinational companies or libraries?

19. Level of customer service and technical support provided. You want someone you can call who is readily available when you have a question or a problem. What things are covered and included with the setup and annual fees you pay and what kind of help costs extra?

20. Is everything routed through the vendor's server? Most of the vendors you encounter will be application service providers (ASP), meaning that they host the software on their server and all transactions are routed through their server. Some libraries have reported that this can slow down response time. Some companies offer you the option of purchasing the software and then you can install it onsite, but this is a very expensive route to go.

21. Will proprietary databases work? This continues to be one of the greatest challenges for all companies who offer the co-browsing feature. You want to make sure you can use all those expensive databases that now consume a major part of your budget. Ask lots of questions about which databases will work and which won't and under what circumstances.

22. Americans with Disabilities Act (ADA) compliance. Computers have made a huge difference in the lives of people who can't come to the library and need to work from home. Most of the software packages you'll consider will be helpful to some degree, but ask if the vendor has given some specific thought to this.

service, you will still need to worry about network issues. The service planning stage must involve a clear understanding of the live reference software configuration and the local network configurations. This can get complicated, so the best scenario would include an information technology person on the planning team who is responsible for direct consultation with the vendor about network concerns. Making your systems group part of the planning process may present challenges, since systems staff and reference librarians often have different perspectives. But it will be worth it. You'll avoid major glitches and end up creating a better service.

ASK THESE QUESTIONS ABOUT SOFTWARE

A checklist of questions to ask yourself, your colleagues, and software vendors appears on the preceeding pages. Use these questions to select the software that will work best for you.

Now we will take a look at how some of the software programs that are being used in libraries relate to the five models of live virtual reference: basic, advanced, homegrown, collaborative, and corporate.

OPTION 1: USE BASIC SOFTWARE

Basic software is simple and inexpensive. Basic software allows librarians and patrons to communicate in real-time with text-messaging through pop-up windows on the World Wide Web. Since the software is inexpensive, a library can get its feet wet with only a modest financial investment. The library can gain experience that will allow an informed decision about whether and how to continue with a more advanced service and more sophisticated software. Two examples of basic software packages in use in libraries that will be discussed here are AOL's Instant Messenger and LivePerson. Another example is LiveAssistance.

> **AOL IM Advantages and Disadvantages**
>
> **Advantages**
> 1. It's free.
> 2. Provides text messaging.
> 3. Readily available as part of the AOL online service, which has over 100 million subscribers (Dunn, 2001).
> 4. Also available as standalone software. You can download and use Instant Messenger without subscribing to AOL.
> 5. Offers Voice over IP (VoIP).
> 6. Supports file sharing.
>
> **Disadvantages**
> 1. Although it comes installed on millions of the computers sold, it still needs to be set up and configured before use.
> 2. Provides no archiving function. In addition, it wasn't designed for reference transactions.
> 3. No co-browsing.
> 4. Free now, but AOL could begin charging in the future.

AOL INSTANT MESSENGER

The great thing about AOL Instant Messenger (also known as AIM or AOL IM or just IM) is that you can download it for free and start doing live virtual reference immediately! That is, as long as you have a staffing model worked out. Still, for getting going quickly, it's hard to beat AOL IM. One big disadvantage is that it requires the user to download and register for the software at their end. Many young adults between the ages of fifteen and twenty-five, however, have already done so and use IM all the time. Patrons older than twenty-five are probably not as familiar with AOL IM.

AOL's Instant Messenger is being used by SUNY Morrisville for their real-time reference service. Librarian Bill Drew reports being pleased with AOL IM and explains: "we consider our service using AOL IM a success even though we get less than one request a day. It costs us nothing except maybe some time, we are able to reach others we may not have reached before, it improves our image by showing us as techno-savvy to our students, it adds to our tools, and we all like it" (Drew, 2001).

In the screen shot in Figure 7–1, notice how the Instant Messenger window has popped up on top of the library's Web page. This is where the librarian and patron will communicate by text-based chat. You can cut and paste URLs into this window, but you cannot push pages or co-browse.

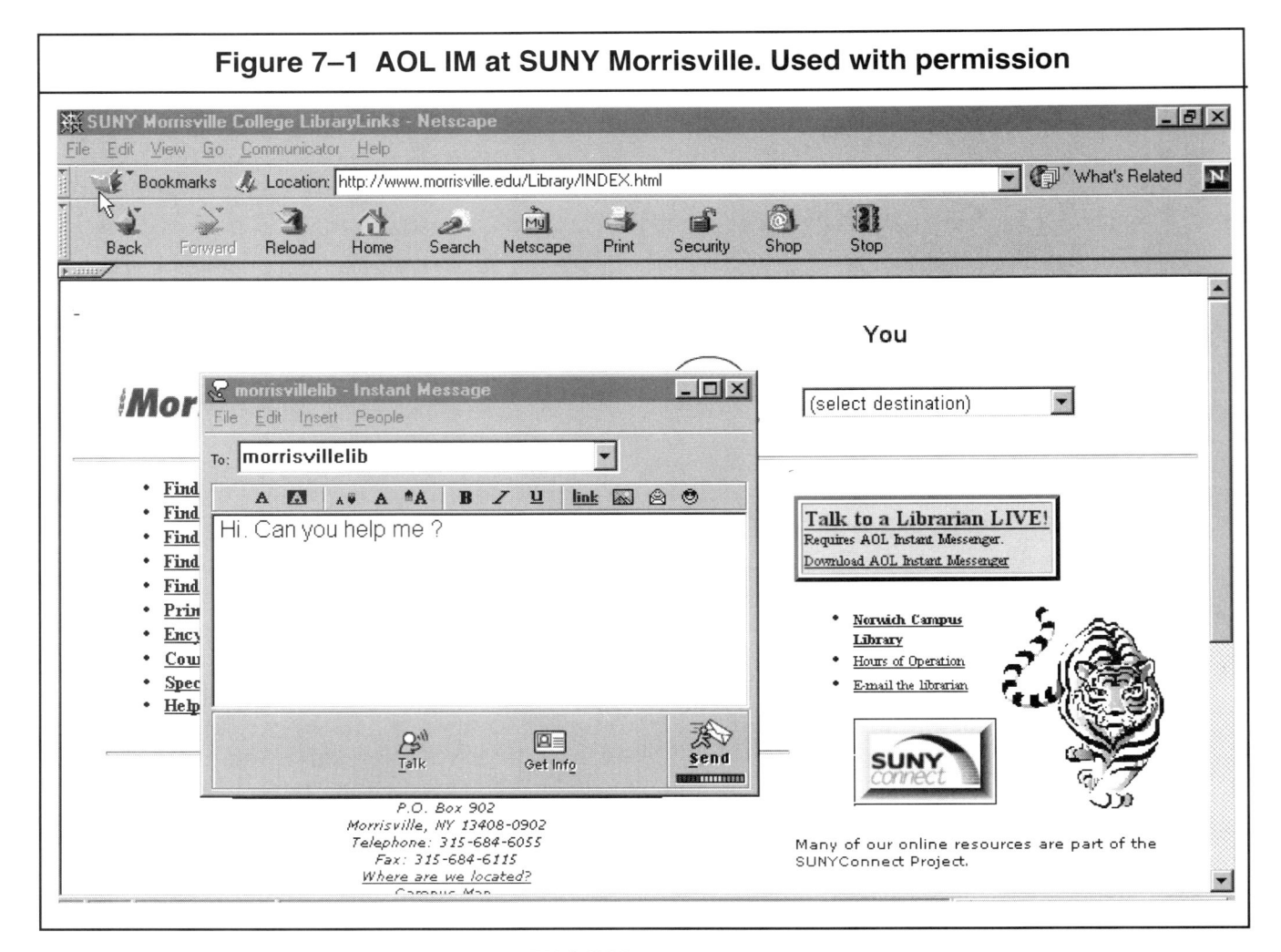

Figure 7–1 AOL IM at SUNY Morrisville. Used with permission

LIVEPERSON

LivePerson is another software package that fits into our basic category. You may see some libraries still using a program called HumanClick, but HumanClick is now a wholly owned subsidiary of LivePerson. LivePerson is not free, but it is not as expensive as other products. Unlike AOL IM, it does have page pushing, but it does not have co-browsing. To use LivePerson the library isn't required to install or run any software on its own server. The LivePerson icon is minimized on the librarian's screen and provides an audio and visual alert when patrons browse into your site or when they ask to chat with you. Patrons can initiate a chat request by clicking on a button on the Web page. A chat window then opens on the user's browser and the librarian receives a "request to chat" alert.

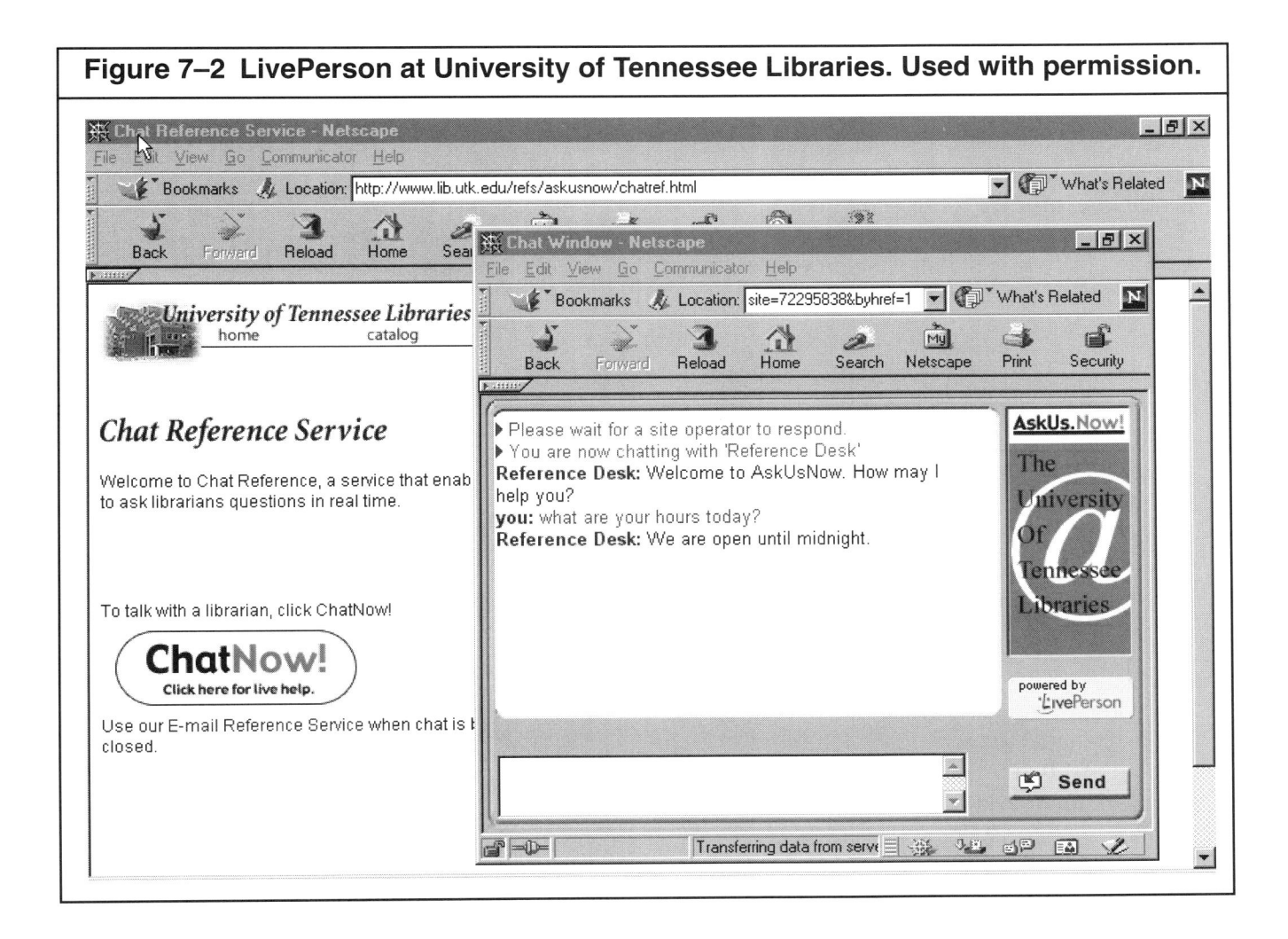

Figure 7–2 LivePerson at University of Tennessee Libraries. Used with permission.

The LivePerson window also gives the librarian a real-time view of a visitor's profile including information such as their host name, pages viewed, and length of visit. When a patron is browsing the library Web site, the librarian may open a pop-up chat box on the visitor's screen at any point and offer him assistance. This feature is like an electronic version of roving reference, but some patrons would probably find it disconcerting and a little spooky to have a librarian suddenly pop up on their screen offering assistance. Use with caution. You don't want to give the patron the feeling that Big Brother is watching.

LivePerson Advantages and Disadvantages

Advantages
1. Easy to use.
2. Minimal training required.
3. The ability to survey users.
4. The ability to e-mail targeted groups of users.
5. Database of canned responses.
6. Call logs (transcripts of sessions) are created.
7. It's Web-based.
8. No additional or special software or plug-ins required.
9. No computing overhead (it's all on the vendor's side).
10. E-mail is generated after hours.
11. More affordable than some higher-end products.
12. Ability to push the patron's browser (page push).
13. Can send active embedded URLs.
14. Supports multiple browsers.
15. Can identify patron by IP address.
16. No difficulty navigating "problem" sites (surveys conflict on this point).

Disadvantages
1. Based on a business model—has an e-commerce, not a library focus.
2. Flexibility of software questionable.
3. Sluggish response time (surveys conflict on this point).
4. Less robust support for Netscape and Macs.
5. Lack of local control.
6. No co-browsing.

(Duke, 2000; Constantine, 2000; Fagan and Calloway, 2001).

OPTION 2: GROW YOUR OWN HOMEGROWN SOFTWARE

Homegrown software is software that has been created by librarians for other librarians. The programs usually use some combination of Linux, PERL, PHP, and MySQL. After the software code has been written, it is usually made available as open source software. Open source software is free for users to download, use, and modify, as long as it remains free for those who ask for it. While attractive to libraries because funding isn't required for a subscription or purchase, it has been slow to catch on because

> **TalkNow Advantages and Disadvantages**
>
> **Advantages**
> 1. Offers text messaging.
> 2. Librarians can logon from any workstation with a Web connection.
> 3. Provides archived conversation logs.
> 4. Can create pre-scripted "canned" messages.
> 5. No special hardware or software required.
> 6. It's free.
>
> **Disadvantages**
> 1. No page pushing.
> 2. No co-browsing.
> 3. No session transcripts available.
> 4. Difficult to download.

high-level technical expertise within the library is required to create and set up the software initially. The library may also remain dependent on that programmer or someone with equal skill to upgrade and maintain the program. Programs written so that some changes can be made using simple means such as a menu can help ameliorate this situation.

Homegrown software has the appeal of being free and outside the mainstream commercial arena. In addition, librarian programmers can customize the software for library needs. The disadvantages are that lots of sweat equity is required to create, implement, maintain, and improve the software. As of this writing, co-browsing is not available with any of the packages. Three libraries are using homegrown software: Temple University, Miami University (Ohio), and Southern Illinois University.

TEMPLE UNIVERSITY

An early adopter of homegrown software was Temple University. Temple University uses a program called TalkNow. TalkNow uses the Linux operating system and a scripting language called PHP. Linux is a flavor of unix, which is becoming increasingly popular. PHP is a server-side, cross-platform HTML embedded scripting language. TalkNow offers text messaging, pre-scripted messages, and archived conversation logs. Page pushing, co-browsing, and transcripts e-mailed to patrons are not available. The program is open source but is difficult to download. Libraries seeking to download open source live virtual reference software should try Miami's or Southern Illinois' software.

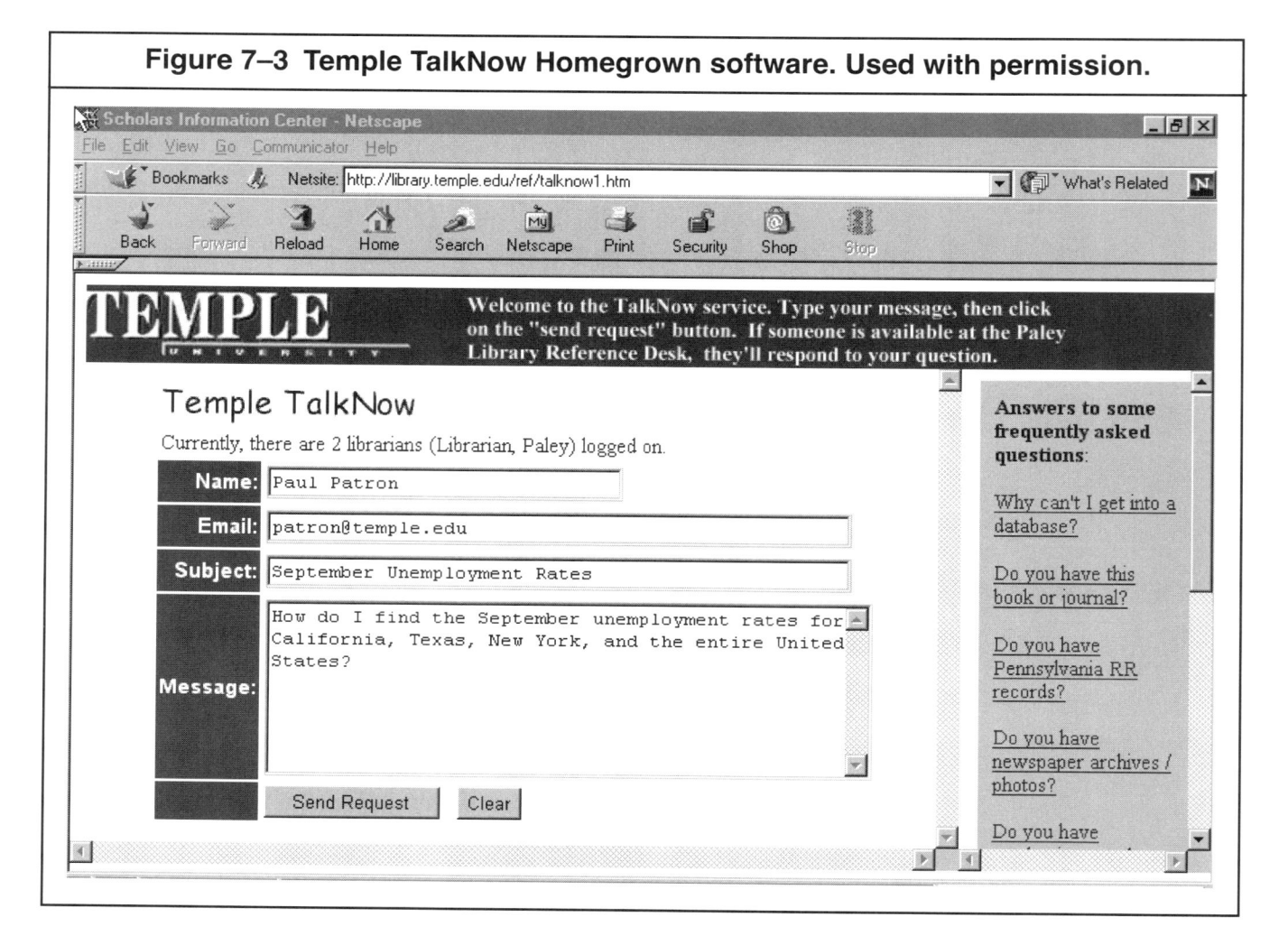

Figure 7-3 Temple TalkNow Homegrown software. Used with permission.

MIAMI UNIVERSITY (OHIO)

Librarian Rob Casson at Miami University Libraries has developed a package called Rakim: A Knowledge Instant Messenger. Rakim uses Linux, PHP, and MySQL. It is similar to many standard chat programs, but includes some enhancements like a shared queue that all librarians can monitor, the ability to refer patrons to specific librarians, and the ability to e-mail transcripts to patrons. Transcripts are useful in helping patrons find resources discussed in the online help sessions.

Rakim is available for download at styro.lib.muohio.edu/rakim/install.html. There is enough documentation that someone with some systems expertise could download it and get it installed. The Miami University Libraries hope to enlist the aid of like-minded librarian programmers who will help to enhance the code and add new features. Rakim is a workable homegrown live vir-

Figure 7–4 Miami University (Ohio) Rakim homegrown software. Used with permission.

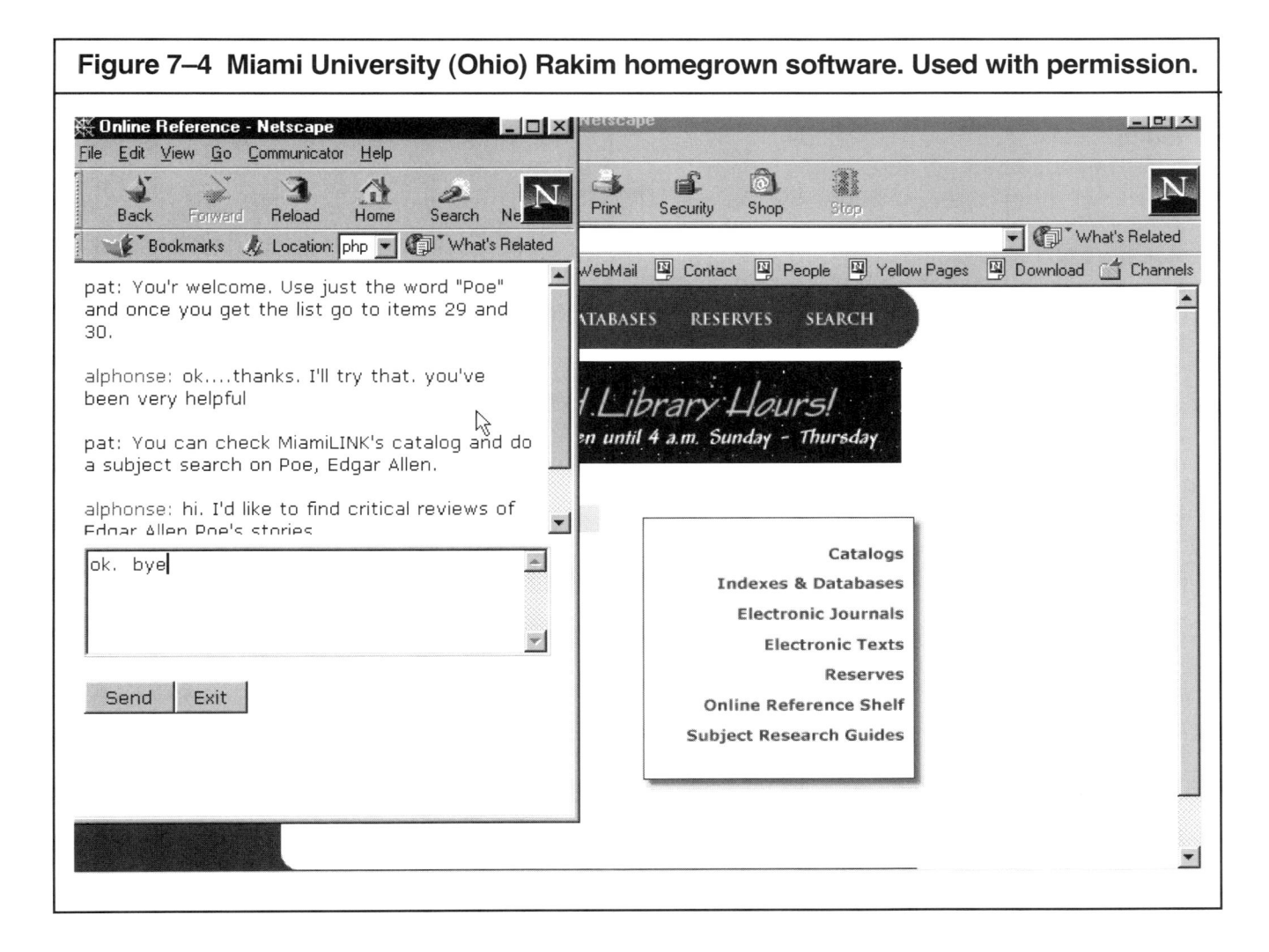

tual reference package. If Rakim could be successfully scaled and features like co-browsing added, it could become a serious competitor to more expensive services such as LSSI (Barr and Webb, 2001).

SOUTHERN ILLINOIS UNIVERSITY

Southern Illinois University (SIU), is another institution experimenting with homegrown software that uses PERL and MySQL and some JavaScript. Librarian Jody Fagan coordinated and managed the project; Keith VanCleave wrote the source code. The service is called Morris Messenger and was launched as a pilot project in the summer of 2001. Software development began in the previous winter of 2000/2001. Other programs such as AOL IM were considered, but SIU didn't want patrons to have to in-

> **Rakim Homegrown Software Advantanges and Disadvantages**
>
> **Advantages**
> 1. Unlimited number of librarians/operators, each with their own login account.
> 2. Shared queue of patrons that all logged in librarians can monitor and take calls from.
> 3. Ability to refer patrons to specific librarians (personal queue).
> 4. Offers text messaging.
> 5. "Page-push"—can cut-n-paste a URL that will be displayed to the patron.
> 6. Audible alert to librarians when there is a new patron in the queue.
> 7. Audible alert to patron when their call is answered.
> 8. Can create shared and personal bookmarks.
> 9. Librarians can customize many settings: ringing, add/delete bookmarks, personal information.
> 10. Transcripts are e-mailed to patron.
>
> **Possible future enhancements:**
> 1. Finishing administrative interfaces: manage system-wide settings.
> 2. Exit surveys.
> 3. Ability to send internal librarian-to-librarian messages to request help and communicate information.
> 4. Voice over IP, which would enable librarians to speak directly to patrons.
>
> **Disadvantages**
> 1. No co-browsing.
> 2. Set-up requires considerable programming expertise.

stall any software. An attempt was made to modify a chat program called Jabber, which would not require patrons to install anything, but it proved too unwieldy.

Morris Messenger accepts input from both staff and patron browsers, saves it to a MySQL database, and then displays the input to the other person's client. Brief lags in the conversation occur because the browser refreshes every 15 seconds and a line that's been typed and sent isn't displayed until a refresh occurs. The patron interface basically just allows the person to enter text. When the conversation is finished, the patron is asked to fill out a short online survey.

Because the data is stored locally, the librarians are able to review the conversation archives, post online surveys, and perform other tests relating to the system. SIU conducted a short online survey during the pilot phase of the project, which generated a large number of responses, and they hope to publish some results from a lengthier user survey. User feedback has been very positive. The only substantive complaints mentioned the limited num-

> **Morris Messenger Homegrown Software Advantages and Disadvantages**
>
> **Advantages**
> 1. Fast response time even if both parties are on a dial-up connection.
> 2. Abilitiy to modify program in response to user needs.
> 3. Ability to ask survey questions.
> 4. Integrates well with other services.
> 5. Can redirect conversations to other online staff.
> 6. Can send active URLs to users.
> 7. Can push pages to the patron's browser.
> 8. Ability to send preformatted (a.k.a. scripted or canned) answers to patrons directly or paste preformatted answers into the input.
> 9. Box for editing before answers are sent.
> 10. Each staff member has personal preformatted answers, nicknames, and buttons.
> 11. Can display the transcript immediately for printing, saving, or e-mail.
>
> **Disadvantages**
> 1. No co-browsing.
> 2. Setup requires considerable programming expertise.

ber of hours. Users want more evening hours, particularly. The challenges SIU faces are familiar to most libraries and include staffing a new service point on an already lean budget and integrating their new live reference service with traditional reference services. The SIU Morris library has made their source code available for download at www.lib.siu.edu/chat/. The system requirements and brief setup instructions are provided. The page also notes that "you will need someone knowledgeable in HTML, PERL and MySQL to install and modify the files." For more information, see "Creating an Instant Messaging Reference System" (Fagan and Calloway, 2001).

OPTION 3: PAY FOR ADVANCED SOFTWARE

As we explained in Chapter 3, software for the Advanced Model of live virtual reference is expensive, full of features, and may have a longer learning curve for some librarians. Advanced software gives you the ability to push Web pages to patrons, co-

> **LSSI Software Advantages and Disadvantages**
>
> **Advantages**
> 1. Designed specifically for libraries.
> 2. Adapts to new technology quickly.
> 3. Offers excellent training.
> 4. Offers chat/text messaging.
> 5. Ability to push the patron's browser (page push).
> 6. Offers co-browsing—all interactions are routed through a proxy server, allowing a librarian and a user to share a single image of a Web page so they can navigate the Web together.
> 7. No special software or hardware required.
> 8. Referral to other librarian on LSSI network.
> 9. Allows librarian and patron to share a Web form.
> 10. Call logs (transcripts of sessions) are created.
> 11. Interview transcript of session is automatically sent to user.
> 12. Users in a queue can be managed and grouped by subject or institution.
> 13. Audio alert to librarians when a patron requests help.
>
> **Disadvantages**
> 1. Co-browsing led to serious problems with certain frame sites, authentication sites, secure sites, personalized sites, and sites requiring plug-ins (the Interact version of the software improves this).
> 2. Complex and can be viewed as hard to use (opinion is mixed on this count, with some librarians also reporting it is easy to use).
> 3. One of the more expensive products.
> 4. Does not send active embedded URLs.
> 5. Does not identify patron by IP address.
>
> (Duke, 2000; Fagan and Calloway, 2001).

browse, offer patrons a list of links visited at the end of the session and e-mail session transcripts. It is the software that can most closely approximate in-person reference, and at times even do things that in-person reference cannot do, such as guide a patron through a search through the Internet. It is the most full-featured software for live virtual reference.

The software in this category is a modified version of eGain customer service software. Library Systems and Services (LSSI) and 24/7 Reference have customized eGain software specifically for libraries. Since both products have eGain software at their base, the interfaces and features of both products are very simi-

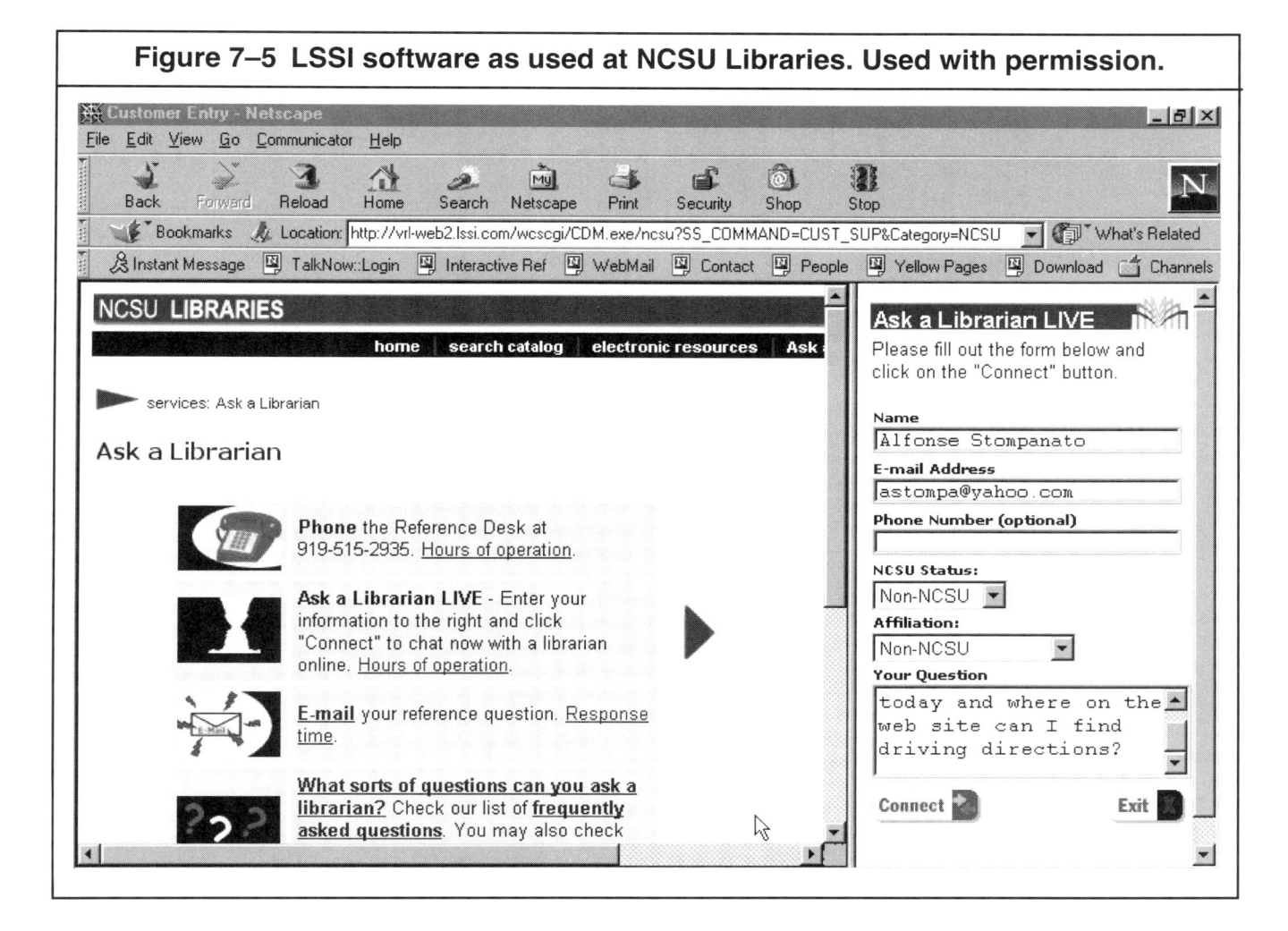

Figure 7–5 LSSI software as used at NCSU Libraries. Used with permission.

lar. One difference is that LSSI is a for-profit company, while 24/7 is a nonprofit organization.

The software provided by LSSI and 24/7 Reference services can be used by a single library or by a consortium. You will most often hear about them in the context of a collaborative arrangement, primarily because they're expensive. But these packages can be used by just one library. The Massachusetts Institute of Technology and North Carolina State University are examples of individual institutions operating live reference services (using LSSI's software) on their own, not as part of a consortium.

LSSI

LSSI is one of the dominant providers of live virtual reference software for libraries. In addition to providing software, LSSI also provides services such as training for librarians and librarians who

> **24/7 Advantages and Disadvantages**
>
> **Advantages**
> 1. Chat.
> 2. Co-browsing.
> 3. Page push.
> 4. Pre-scripted messages.
> 5. Multiple simultaneous sessions.
> 6. Individual software customization.
> 7. Transfer users.
> 8. Session transcripts.
> 9. Statistics.
>
> **Disadvantages**
> 1. Expensive.
> 2. Can have a longer learning curve for some librarians.

are available to answer overflow questions. LSSI has developed a reputation for a willingness to work with customers and accommodate customer needs. Steve Coffman is the vice-president of product development for their Virtual Reference Service. Coffman has been frequently featured at conferences and library events over the past couple of years and has achieved considerable name recognition for LSSI. He has also published a number of articles that have generated lively and heated discussions about the future of libraries in general and reference services in particular. LSSI offers one of the most full-featured packages and also one of the most expensive. Costs will vary from institution to institution and of course will change over time. Contact LSSI (www.virtualreference.net/virtual/) for their most recent price quote.

One of the most attractive features of LSSI's software is the ability of the librarian to have their chat conversation on the right-hand side of the screen, while the librarian can push Web pages to the left-hand side of the screen, such as in Figure 7–5 from North Carolina State University. On the left-hand screen, the librarian has pushed directions to the library. On the right-hand side, the librarian and patron engage in text-based chat.

24/7 REFERENCE

The software provided by 24/7 is almost identical to LSSI, as it is also based on eGain software. The Metropolitan Cooperative Library System (MCLS), a large library consortium located in southern California, received a grant to develop a digital reference

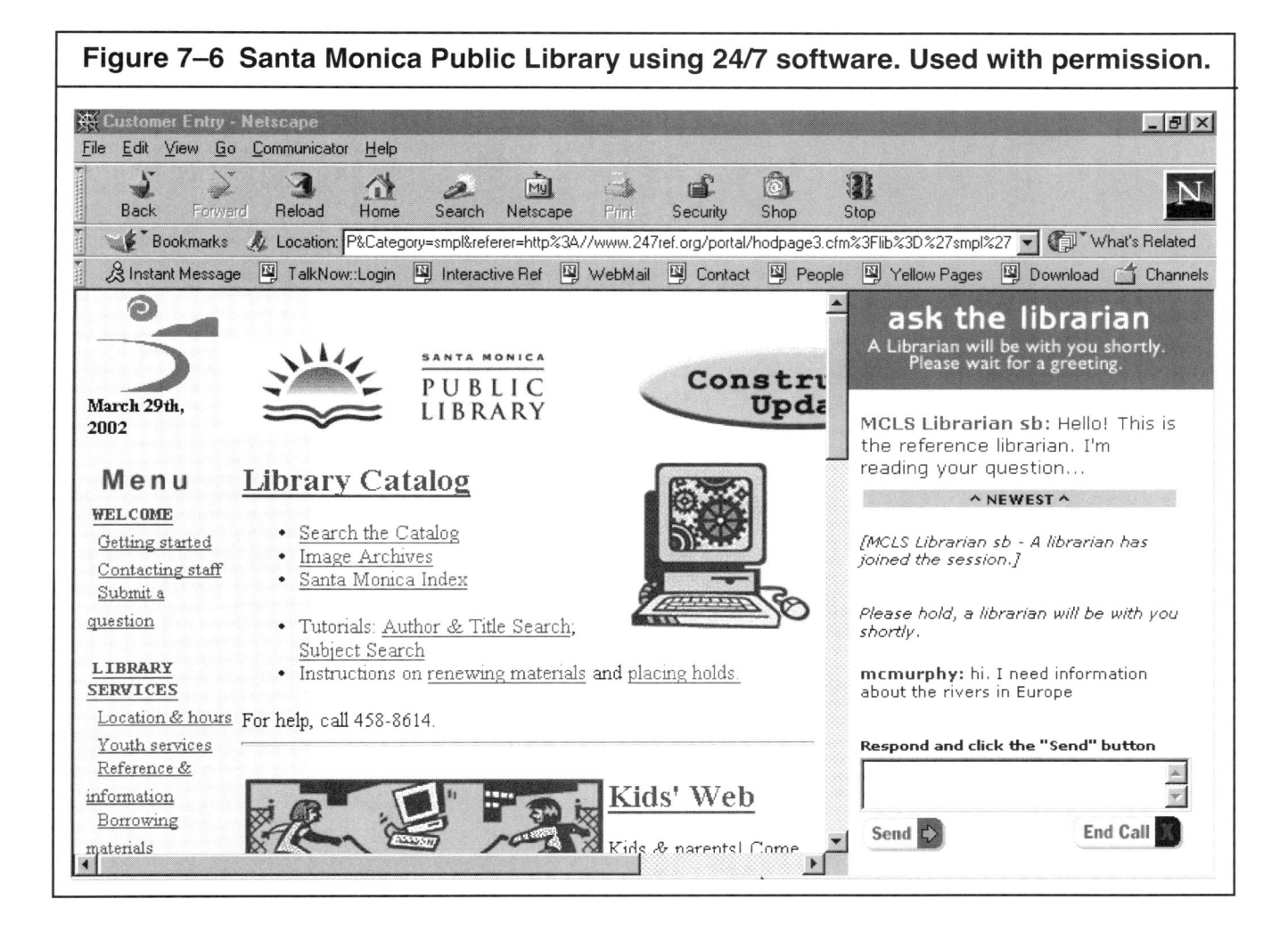

Figure 7–6 Santa Monica Public Library using 24/7 software. Used with permission.

service for its 32 public library members. The goal was to provide libraries with the tools they needed to do live reference on the Web. After initially exploring several different products, they recognized that eGain could be modified and customized to meet the specialized needs of libraries. Over a two year period, they developed and tested a software package that is now available.

They rolled out the new service in MCLS member libraries and then began to market it more widely to other interested libraries. The revenue derived from other non-MCLS libraries helps to support the ongoing MCLS project. One of the differences between 24/7 and LSSI is that 24/7 is a nonprofit organization (although they've partnered with the for-profit Cherry Hill Company to develop the software). Above (Figure 7–6) is an example of 24/7 software being used by the Santa Monica Public Library. Note how similar it looks to LSSI's product.

> **Collaborative Software Advantages and Disadvantages**
>
> **Advantages**
> 1. Cost of the software can be shared.
> 2. Many more librarians are available for staffing.
> 3. Affords an opportunity to build relationships among libraries and librarians.
> 4. Creates a greater pool of expertise for referrals.
>
> **Disadvantages**
> 1. Planning and implementation take longer.
> 2. Scheduling is much more complex.
> 3. Special coordinator is required.
> 4. Must develop global policies for entire group.
> 5. Must develop cost and labor sharing models.

OPTION 4: SHARE COSTS WITH COLLABORATIVE SOFTWARE

When considering what software to choose, there's another approach that is in keeping with the long tradition of cooperation among libraries. A number of libraries offer live virtual reference as part of a consortium. This approach doesn't require any specific software package. Examples of software currently being used by consortiums are LSSI, 24/7, LivePerson, and NetAgent.

Collaborative arrangements spread the cost over the entire group, making it more affordable, but adds the additional challenge of coordinating efforts among many libraries. Using this model means that the individual libraries don't have to go through the often painstaking process of evaluating software. Representatives of the group choose the software, which is then made available to participating libraries.

The collaborative approach is likely to become increasingly popular for at least two reasons. First, many of the most sophisticated software packages with the most advanced features are too expensive for individual libraries to subscribe to or purchase. Second, many libraries don't have sufficient staff to cover more than a few hours a day, which means that the service can't really advance much beyond being an interesting novelty. By pooling resources, libraries can have access to dozens of librarians, rather than just a few. Figure 7–7 is an example of Q and A NJ, the collaborative service based in New Jersey that uses LSSI software.

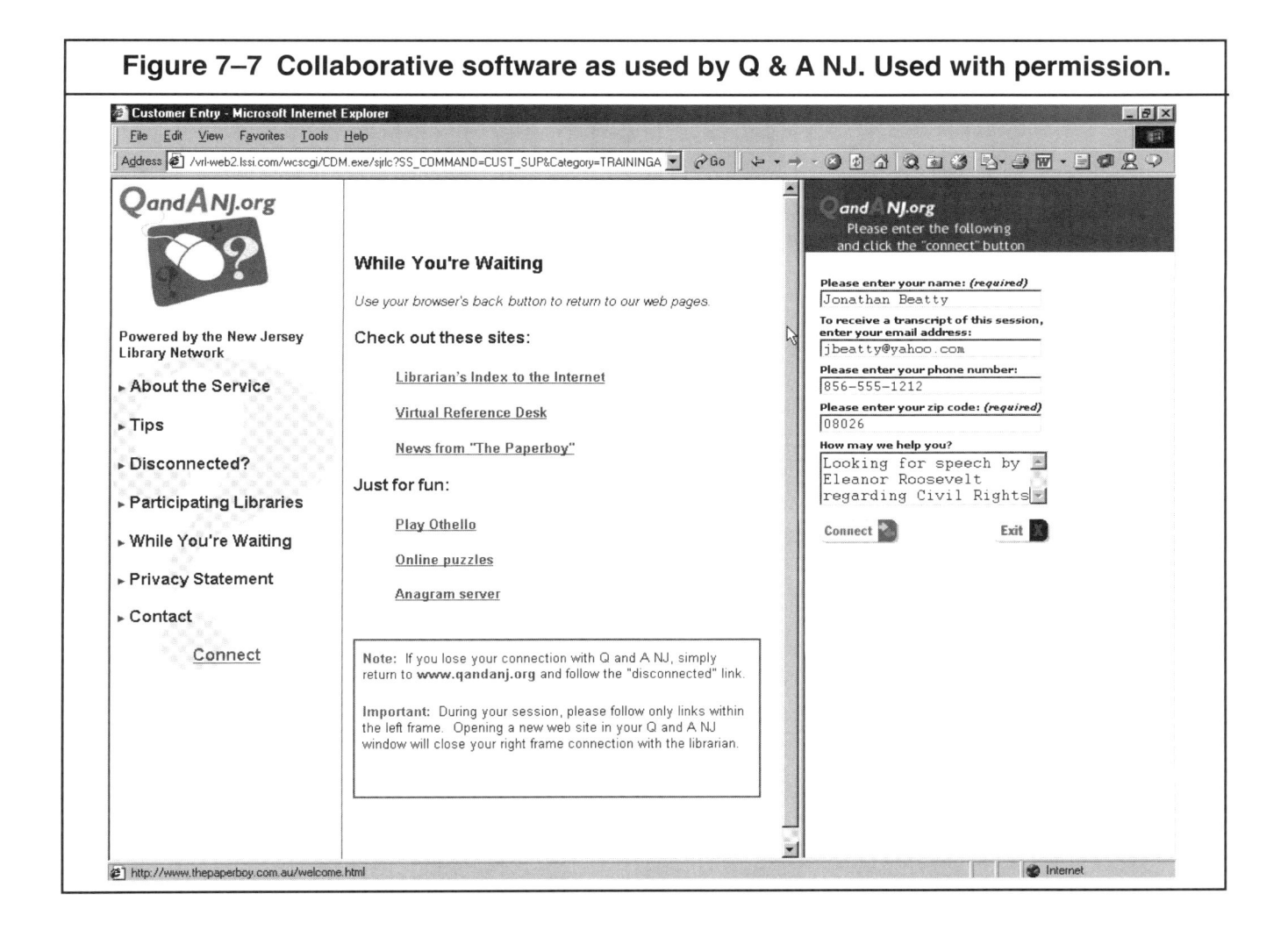

Figure 7–7 Collaborative software as used by Q & A NJ. Used with permission.

OPTION 5: MONITOR CORPORATE SOFTWARE DEVELOPMENTS

As we've discussed, it's useful to keep an eye on what's happening in the corporate world, because that's where most software is first developed and then eventually filters down to libraries. The idea is not so much that libraries will replicate corporate call centers, but rather that librarians need to stay abreast of leading edge technology so they can begin thinking about library-specific applications.

The notion of giving patrons multiple access points to access reference help has evolved over time in libraries. Telephone reference was added to in-person service many years ago. E-mail reference has actually been in use in some libraries since the 1980s. Web forms came into use during the mid 1990s and chat reference started showing up as a library service in the late 1990s. Each of these new services was simply added to the existing array of access points, giving patrons more choices when they needed help.

An ongoing goal among companies who create customer relationship management software is to build products that offer the customer multiple access points. Customers can contact the company in the way that suits them best. A number of software packages have attempted to integrate various types of customer interaction including e-mail, voice, chat, and Web forms. RightNow Web 4.0 offers customers the opportunity to select answers from pull-down menus or they can search a knowledge base by entering keywords. If users can't find what they're looking for this way, they can send an e-mail message to an agent or initiate a text chat session with them. The user's question can be routed to the most appropriate agent by using the keywords in the search. For instance, if the user mentions a particular product, the question is routed to the agent who's an expert on that product (Hollman, 2001).

Another software package, eSupport, offers three options to help customers locate information. Repeat customers can simply enter their questions and eSupport's natural language search engine will display answers from the company's knowledge base. This package can also display a list of FAQs to customers, which helps to educate them about the products, and they can click on a question to view the solution. Finally, there's a link that allows customers to e-mail agents if they still need help and all three options can be combined on a single Web page. This kind of integrated software has begun to filter down to libraries. RefTracker is a product offered by LSSI as part of the Virtual Reference Toolkit that integrates e-mail, desk, and phone reference with online reference (Coffman, 2002).

Another area of development that has gotten a lot of attention is the knowledge base. A knowledge base is created from customer questions and answers. It's an extension of the familiar Frequently Asked Questions Web page. The questions and answers that occur often are stored in a database and made available for future inquiries by customers. Companies hope that customers will be able to use the knowledge base to answer a majority, say 80 percent, of all their questions. Customers will go to the knowledge base first, in a self-service fashion. Only if that doesn't work will they move on to the more expensive live help service.

Voice over IP (VoIP) is another hot discussion topic, but big installations are few and far between. The launch of Dow Chemical Company's new IP converged network may be a milestone in the development of IP telephony. All the big corporate players will be watching as this Fortune 500 giant rolls out its 50,000 user integrated IP voice/data network (Wexler, 2002). This project may provide the confidence level needed for other large corporations to jump on the bandwagon. Part of the project includes the deployment of IP-based multimedia applications through regional Web-based call centers.

The corporate call center is a much different environment than that found in most libraries, but many of the software features that libraries want and will need for live virtual reference will be developed here first. You should make it a point to add customer relationship management software developments to your personal current awareness program.

SUMMARY

Selecting software is a big decision, and the multitude of programs available can make the choice confusing. One way to simplify the decision is to classify the software into the five models of live virtual reference. One thing is certain: software programs will change. The features will change, the companies will change, and the prices will change. Use the checklist in this chapter to evaluate software programs for yourself, and don't forget to involve your systems staff.

Furthermore, remember that you can always change your decision, especially if you've chosen one of the more basic packages. Once you have decided on a staffing model and selected your software, you are ready to start implementing your live virtual reference service.

REFERENCES

Barr, Belinda, and Kathleen Webb. 2001 79 Peas in a Pod: Developing a Virtual Reference Service for the OhioLINK Consortium. Paper presented at conference, VRD 2001 Conference, 13 November.

Chudnov, Daniel. 1999. "Open Source Software: The Future of Library Systems?" *Library Journal* 124, no. 13.

Coffman, Steve. 2001. "Distance Education and Virtual Reference: Where Are We Headed?" *Computers in Libraries* 21 no. 4.

Coffman, Steve. DIG_REF 2002. Accessed 3/12/02.

Constantine, Paul. 2000. Cornell University's Live Help Service: In the Virtual Reference Desk Second Annual Digital Reference Conference Proceedings [Online]. Available: www.vrd.org/conferences/VRD2000/proceedings/constantine-intro.shtml [2001, November 23].

Drew, Bill. DIG_REF, 12/10/01. Accessed: 1/28/02.

Duke University. 2000. Live On Line Reference [Online]. Available: www.lib.duke.edu/reference/liveonlineref.htm#Evaluation [2002, February 2].

Dunn, Katie. 2001. "Instant Online Messages Let Fingers Do the Talking" *Insight on the News* 17, no. 31.

Fagan, Jody Condit, and Michele Calloway. 2001. "Creating an Instant Messaging Reference System" *Information Technology and Libraries* 20 (4) December. Available online: www.lita.org/ital/ital2004.html#anchor250046.

Francoeur, Stephen. 2001. The Teaching Librarian [Online]. Available: pages.prodigy.net/tabo1/digref.htm [November 20, 2001].

Hollman, Lee. 2001. "A Ready Reference for Your Customers." *Call Center Magazine* 14, no. 5.

Tiazkun, Scott. 2001. "eGain: Taking the Customer's Point of View" IDC Report (November).

Wexler, Joanie. 2002. "Dow Blazes VOIP Trail" *Computerworld* 36, no. 4.

PART III

IMPLEMENTING AND INCORPORATING LIVE VIRTUAL REFERENCE

8 TRAINING THE STAFF FOR LIVE VIRTUAL REFERENCE

We have come a long way. We have covered the essential background and planning aspects of live virtual reference. You know what live virtual reference is and isn't, and why you may or may not want to do it. You know the five models of live virtual reference and picked one that applies to your situation. You've initiated the planning process, and have resolved how you are going to deal with staffing. You've picked software and figured out how to pay for it, if necessary. You should have resolved some of the major questions of policy. If you have taken your institution through these steps, you are finally ready for actually implementing your own version of live virtual reference at your institution. Three final hurdles remain: training, launch and marketing, and evaluating.

Throughout this book we have maintained that live virtual reference is a new service that is rooted in traditional reference librarianship. Don't forget this when it comes to training. It's true that live virtual reference uses new technology and that you will have to train your reference staff in the mechanics of using the new software. But answering live virtual reference questions is still answering reference questions: your reference librarians still need traditional core reference skills. A live virtual reference librarian without traditional reference skills is no librarian at all. How much training you provide will in part depend on the person to be trained. If a librarian is already familiar with Internet chat and multitasking, they may not need much training on software mechanics. They may however have much to learn about print reference sources. Other librarians may need a while to get used to communicating by chat and operating with so many windows open. Training will also vary depending on the model of live virtual reference you have chosen. In this chapter, we outline the general skills and proficiencies needed for all the models, then discuss each model individually.

GENERAL SKILLS FOR ALL MODELS

The skills and proficiencies that apply to all the live virtual reference models fall into four areas:

- Core reference skills
- Real-time chat techniques
- Software specific skills
- Live virtual reference policies

CORE REFERENCE SKILLS

The better trained your librarians are in core reference skills, the better they will be at live virtual reference, period. There are no shortcuts. Of course, training in these skills goes well beyond the scope of this book. Your librarians should begin to acquire these skills in library school and then develop them over a career of reference practice with the help of librarian mentors. We understand core reference skills to include:

- In-depth knowledge of print and electronic sources
  Why an in-depth knowledge of print sources? Many live virtual reference patrons will come to you only after they have searched the Internet and found nothing. That means there's a good chance that what they're looking for isn't on the Internet, so you'll have to know print sources and how to find them as well as Internet sources. Of course you have to know electronic sources (Web sites and subscription databases) too, because there's also a good chance the patron didn't find anything because they weren't searching correctly, or weren't searching in the right place. For good advice on using the Internet in reference work see Michael Sauers' book *Using the Internet as a Reference Tool: A How-To-Do-it Manual for Librarians*.
- Ability to conduct searches using advanced search techniques
  You need knowledge of search techniques because it's a basic reference skill, but also for the same reason you need knowledge of sources: virtual patrons will come to you after they have tried ineffectual searches or that have resulted in zero hits. Finding results quickly means knowing how to perform sophisticated keyword and subject searches in a multiplicity of search tools.
- Evaluate sources for authority and bias
  We all know that everything in print or on the Internet isn't always true or free of bias, but our patrons aren't always aware of this. Live virtual reference doesn't mean sending a patron to any old Web site, it means providing them with high-quality information, whatever the source. If necessary, have your librarians brush up on techniques on evaluating Web sites. When providing live virtual ref-

erence, suggest that your librarians begin with Web sources that have already been vetted by librarians, such as Librarians' Index to the Internet (www.lii.org/) or a similar source. See also Sauers (2001).
- Expertise in the art of conducting reference interviews
The need to conduct reference interviews doesn't stop just because reference is on the Web. Helping patrons figure out what it is they really want is just as important in the virtual environment as in the physical environment. The real-time element of live virtual reference that allows live reference interviews to take place is one of the reasons you are offering live virtual reference over e-mail virtual reference in the first place. Don't forget the old techniques you use at the physical desk. Since the mode of communication is different, however, you will have to learn some new techniques. The next section explains these techniques.

REAL-TIME CHAT TECHNIQUES

Reference interviews are tricky enough face-to-face. In the virtual environment, they're even trickier. In live virtual reference, there are no visual and oral cues, communication is mediated through software, and reference is taking place on the World Wide Web, where users have different expectations. These differences make virtual communication more complicated than face-to-face communication.

The lack of visual and oral cues in virtual reference means that the chance for miscommunication is greater. Neither person can make eye contact, use facial expressions, or get information from body language. Reference librarians won't be able to tell just by looking if a patron is bright-eyed and enthusiastic or frustrated and tired. The patron won't be able to see that the librarian is interested in their question and taking action toward its resolution. Emotional subtleties communicated through the nuances of tone of voice are gone. We take for granted the tremendous amount of information that flows through visual and oral cues. When communication suddenly takes place without them, the chance for confusion is increased. Don't underestimate the differences between chat reference and face-to-face reference. There is a definite skill set that needs to be acquired and a set of techniques that can be learned. Use the following real-time chat techniques.

- Use short, frequent messages, but don't blather on.
  Chat communication has been compared to Morse code—

think short bursts of activity. If you try to compose a three paragraph masterpiece, it will appear to the other side that you are ignoring them. Use short, informative messages instead. Remember: the patron cannot see what you are doing. Explain what is happening on your end. Give them frequent updates as to what you are doing so they know you are involved in their question. Silence is to be avoided, and composing long messages means silence. If you must give a long response, separate it into smaller messages so that the patron can read the first part of your response while you compose the second. You can use ellipsis (...) to let the patron know that more information is coming. Examples

I'm working on your question...
I'm sending you a Web page...
Can you hold on a moment?

- Learn how to type, but don't sweat a few typos.
  The necessity to compose quick, short messages means that real-time chat has a greater intensity and more time pressure than physical desk reference. To facilitate quick responses, librarian typing skills must be up to snuff. Hunt and peck typists won't last long in this medium. Spelling and grammar should not be so atrocious that you embarrass yourself and your institution, but don't get too worried if you make a few typos. The important thing is to get your message across so you can be understood. Should you use a spell checker? We don't recommend it; too time consuming.
- Drop the formality, but don't get too cute.
  Many people think of written communication as having a higher level of formality than oral communication, so they take longer to think and compose their sentences as if they will be written in stone. Not so in Internet chat. Don't agonize over your words before you hit the send button. Chat is more akin to a quick conversation than a formal letter or essay. Type like you speak. Be informal and friendly; keep up your end of the dialogue. Watch out, though. Since tone is difficult to convey over chat, stay away from feeble attempts at humor that have a good chance of being misinterpreted. Some chatters use emoticons—symbols with happy faces—to express humor and other emotions, but you can overdo it with these too. Fall back on your professionalism and avoid being misinterpreted.

- Be concise, but don't be rude.
  Conversations that occur through Internet chat can actually take longer than in-person interactions. Several minutes can be required to exchange a few sentences. Crisp, clear, concise sentences are preferred so as not to waste everyone's time. Once miscommunication occurs, it can take a long time to clear things up, to the point that a phone call may be required. Aim for clarity and avoid phrase constructions that have even the potential to be obfuscatory. There's a difference between being concise and being rude, however. Yes or no one-word answers may be interpreted by some patrons as brusque and impolite.
- Use scripted messages, but don't become librario-bot.
  Scripted messages allow you to send messages that you have already typed beforehand. Common expressions that can be used over and over—hello, how can I help you—save typing time. Be careful, however, that you don't start sounding like a robot. The whole point of live virtual reference is that the patron gets to speak to a real, live person. Make sure you are listening to their questions and responding appropriately. If patrons get the feeling they are talking to an automaton, "live" reference is no longer very "alive" at all.
- Multitask, but don't crash your computer or brain.
  Live virtual reference and a multitask mindset go well together. Having a general orientation toward doing more than one thing at a time is a big help. You'll need to keep one eye on the chat window, one eye on a Web search, another eye on a database search, and another eye on a page in a reference book. Hone your general windows proficiency—copying and pasting, minimizing and maximizing, saving and sending files. Develop the dexterity to jump around between multiple open windows and keep them all straight. While one Web page is loading you can be doing another search in another browser window. Having multiple browsers and applications running allows you to save time and get information to your patron quicker. Of course having multiple applications running can also be confusing. You may get mixed up and send your patron the wrong page, or forget where you are. Your computer may not like it either. Too many applications may cause your machine to run slower, or in the worst case scenario, to freeze and crash. You'll lose the connection with your patron and have to reboot. If you are not a natural multitasker, practice getting used to it, and know what to do when something goes wrong.

> **Real-Time Chat Techniques Checklist**
>
> - Use short frequent messages, but don't blather on
> - Learn how to type, but don't sweat a few typos
> - Drop the formality, but don't get too cute
> - Be concise, but don't be rude
> - Use scripted messages, but don't become librario-bot
> - Multitask, but don't crash your computer or brain

SOFTWARE SPECIFIC SKILLS

Software specific skills include all procedures and features that must be mastered to answer a call using the specific software the library has chosen to use. Specific skills training is training on which keyboard operations result in the desired outcomes. Procedures and instructions should be written down and clearly understandable. Software specific features include:

- How to log in
- How to recognize that a question has come in
- How to answer a question
- How to close a session
- How to log out
- Simple technical fixes

LIVE VIRTUAL REFERENCE POLICIES

Part of the planning process for live virtual reference is drafting policy (see Chapter 4). By now, you should have made enough policy decisions so that you can begin answering questions. Don't worry about trying to cover every contingency. You can't. You can add and modify your policy as you go along. Whatever policy decisions you or the planning committee has agreed upon, make sure the librarians who are answering live virtual reference know what they are. They need to know who the intended audience is for the service and what to do if they receive a question from outside that audience. They need to know what level of service or how long to spend with each patron. They need to know what the policy is on document delivery, what the appropriate tools for live virtual reference are, and what the privacy policy is. All of these policy decisions should be documented and available through a Web site.

> **Live Virtual Reference Policies**
>
> - Audience
> - Level of service
> - Document delivery
> - Appropriate tools
> - Patron privacy

We have just covered the areas of training that apply to the five models of live virtual reference: core reference skills, real-time chat techniques, software specific skills, and live virtual reference policies. Now it's time to look more closely at how these areas can be applied specifically to the five models.

TRAINING FOR THE BASIC MODEL

As you may recall, the guiding philosophy behind the basic model is minimalism. Minimal cost, minimal scheduling, minimal planning, minimal software—and minimal training. Minimal training means at least a one-hour session, but it could be done in less, especially if your librarians are already familiar with chat. Most learning will occur on the job, as live virtual reference questions come in. In the one-hour session you need to go over at least three of the four areas of training—real-time chat techniques, software specific skills, and live virtual reference policies. As for core reference skills, you will simply assume or take for granted the reference skills your librarians already have.

In the one-hour session, you will have to communicate and give a demonstration of the real-time chat techniques. If you have librarians who are already familiar with chat, ask them to volunteer to demonstrate how to carry on a conversation. Encourage librarians who are unfamiliar with chat to practice with each other. Provide a handout with the chat techniques on them. When questions start coming in, look for librarians who are having difficulty and deal with them on a case-by-case basis.

In the basic model, the software should be straightforward enough on the librarian side that librarians can use it without too much difficulty. Still, the basic features will need to be explained. The bare minimum that needs to be communicated in the basic training session is how to log in, how to recognize that a question has come in, how to answer a question, how to close a session,

> **Checklist for Basic Model Training**
>
> - Minimal training
> - One-hour session
> - Most training occurs as questions come in
> - Deal with individual problems on a case-by case basis

and how to log out. This should all be done in a hands-on session with a simulated question and answer. In addition, instructions for these procedures should be written down and kept in a notebook or policy manual. Any known bugs or simple technical problems that can be fixed relatively easily should also be included. The full brunt of the practice time, however, will occur as the service is operating and librarians answer real questions. Training in the basic model is training as-you-go-along. As long as the basic features are explained, you can deal with problems as they come up. The benefit is that you won't have to spend a lot of time training, and librarians who don't like training or being trained can be allowed to figure things out for themselves.

The final component in the basic model training is to make sure that all question answerers are informed and aware of live reference policies. In accord with the basic model's minimalism, live reference policies should be similar to desk reference policies. Any policies that can be transferred from the physical desk to the virtual desk should be transferred. Any policies that diverge from the desk should be explained. This is a good time to go over all reference policies—user group, level of service, philosophy of reference, document delivery, appropriate tools, and patron confidentiality. Areas that often need particular attention in live reference are the accepted user group, the level of service, and patron confidentiality. Librarians should also know who to contact if a technical problem occurs that they cannot solve on their own.

TRAINING FOR THE HOMEGROWN MODEL

The homegrown model is similar to the basic model except the software used is not a commercial product. Training for the homegrown model should follow the same rough outline as the basic

> **Checklist for Homegrown Model Training**
>
> - Similar to basic model
> - Quirks or irregularities
> - Technical workarounds
> - Programming and installation skills

model: it should include the real-time chat techniques, the software specific skills, and the live virtual reference policies. Since the software is not a commercial product, however, more time may need to be allotted to particular quirks of the software. Particular attention should be paid to anything different about the features that needs to be explained, small technical glitches that need to be worked around, or features unique to the software.

Since one of the main benefits of open source software is the ability to modify the software, librarians should be trained to be alert to possible changes in the software that could make the product better. The open source model really only works if you have someone on staff who is willing to spend some time working with the source code. If you are lucky enough to have such a person, that person should be encouraged to build on their open source programming skills by attending workshops and courses. More and more systems librarians are becoming interested in programming and open source code; they should be encouraged and trained. Reference librarians who are looking for new projects may also want to increase their technical skills and even move into the systems side of librarianship if given the opportunity. Valuable skills for open source operations include networking, server administration, Perl, MySql, php, and unix.

TRAINING FOR THE ADVANCED MODEL

Extensive staff training is part of the advanced model. Training includes all the topics covered in the basic session but everything is more formalized. In the basic model, training occurs live, while the service is actually up, baptism-by-fire style. In the advanced model, instead of live training, training consists of exercises conducted by a formal trainer. The exercises are designed to illustrate and give librarians practice with the special features of the software. Since the software has more features, and since the library is paying more money for those features, more training is

> **Checklist for Advanced Model Training**
>
> - Real-time chat techniques
> - Formalized training exercises using real sample questions
> - Formalized practice time
> - Software specific skills
> - Focus on advanced features such as page pushing
> - Live virtual reference policies

necessary to ensure that librarians know about the features and use them. Short of real live question answering, sustained practice using real questions is the best way for librarians to get the hang of integrating the new tools into their reference routine. Examples of real questions can be obtained from the software vendor, taken from the library physical reference desk or e-mail reference desk, or from places on the Web that post their questions with identifying information stripped. Besides general questions, be sure to customize some to your library-specific environment.

For the more expensive software packages, training can involve pre-training exercises, a full one-day hands-on training session with a trainer, plus post-training exercises. In order to get your librarians to practice, schedule required practice time. If librarians continue to have questions after the training period, a customer service representative may be available by telephone. This kind of extensive training spares in-house librarians from having to draw up training exercises, and probably means your staff will be trained more thoroughly. Of course all this training comes with a price, usually built into the price of the software. Another disadvantage is that some librarians have bristled at being forced to spend so much time training on software in addition to their other responsibilities. If the software changes frequently, as is often the case with the advanced packages, librarians will have to continue to learn about the new features.

TRAINING FOR THE COLLABORATIVE MODEL

The collaborative model is a variation on the advanced model. Libraries pool their resources to purchase the expensive software and share the staffing burden. Training consists of everything in

> **Checklist for Training for the Collaborative Model**
>
> - Real-time chat techniques
> - Software specific skills
> - Live virtual reference policies
> - Coordinate training at central location
> - Set up a listserv for communication
> - A Web page can bring together various service policies and resources

the advanced model, but is made even more complicated by the dispersed locations of the librarians and the differing policies, databases, and catalogs of the participating libraries.

The scattered nature of the librarians will make training all the participating librarians more difficult to coordinate. A project coordinator with good organizing skills will have to schedule the training sessions and make sure everyone attends. Project managers at individual libraries can coordinate activity at the library level. Web-based calendars such as Yahoo Calendar (www.calendar.yahoo.com) can be used so that all members have access to an up-to-date schedule. Practice training may be done virtually to lessen the impact of the different locations. Some collaborative reference groups have done all their training and yet have never even been in the same room together.

The fact that librarians are at different locations means that a way for all the libraries to communicate will have to be worked into training. Set up a listserv for all the participating members and make sure everyone is subscribed. Have members use the list to make announcements, share techniques, and vent frustrations. Another possibility, if your software permits it and your librarians are up for it, is chat meetings.

A distinguishing feature of the collaborative model is that libraries answer questions from patrons of other participating libraries. This can get hairy for librarians if the question involves searching another library's catalog, knowing what databases member libraries subscribe to or not, and knowing the policies. For most librarians, it's enough to have to know their own library, the thought of knowing ten or fifteen or more libraries can be terrifying. Many of the existing collaborative services really function as separate questioning answering services, so the problem of referring patrons back to their own library doesn't come up as much as one might expect. When it does, it helps to have a Web page that is a way for librarians to access the policies and catalogs of participating libraries quickly.

TRAINING FOR THE CORPORATE MODEL

In Chapter 3, we claimed that libraries could learn a great deal by keeping up with trends in e-commerce and corporate call centers. The area of training is no exception. You may be surprised to learn that corporate call centers deal with issues similar to those that confront libraries—retaining online customers in the face of competition from Web sites, moving from over-the-counter to online selling, balancing calls that take one minute with calls that take 15 minutes, having multiple levels of agents for handling simple to advanced questions. The most enlightened companies view training their online operators as an essential part of a strategy to increase profitability and market share. Some of the less enlightened companies, however, are no better than electronic sweatshops when it comes to their employees. Training in the corporate model can mean saving money because it reduces staff turnover; better trained agents are more likely to attract and retain customers. Believe it or not, some companies with call centers are very interested in training their operators and have developed some advanced methods for doing it.

One training trend in corporate call centers is technology based training or e-learning (Read, 2001). Training occurs through the desktop with interactive Web-based modules that include text, audio and video clips, and animated cartoons. Some believe these modules lead to more retention of information and fewer agent errors than classroom training. The lesson or video can be replayed by the agent when necessary; a supervisor can cue up a lesson immediately after an agent has had a difficult call; and the modules can be customized and targeted to the operators' deficiencies. From a cost saving point of view, training can be scheduled during the down times of slow call volume and eliminate the necessity and cost of taking customer service agents to an expensive classroom (Read, 2001).

Although e-learning is popular, others believe that it must be complemented or blended with classroom training with live instructors for full effectiveness (Throne, 2001). Classroom training gives operators more opportunity to get feedback from an instructor and from other classmates. Some human encounter communication skills are better transmitted in person. Companies have weekly sessions in which operators are updated on changes in products and are given time to practice. These companies view online learning as a supplement and a way to reduce the total hours of classroom instruction, but not the be-all and end-all of training.

Corporate Model Training Trends
• Technology based e-learning • Blended learning • Supervisor training • Niche training • Not sink or swim but integrate training with practice

Other corporate trends include training for supervisors in coaching and management skills, niche training, and an integrated approach to teaching and applying what is taught. Supervisors are trained to be good coaches who help trainees be adult learners instead of just making them feel like they are wrong (Read, 2001). Niche training refers to the realization that the skill sets for e-mail, phone, and Web chat are different and one person may be better at specializing in one than trying to do all three. An integrated approach to training means that training and actual practice complement each other, and the company doesn't force the agent to sink or swim by learning on the job.

SUMMARY

The skills needed to answer live virtual reference questions are rooted in the traditional core reference skills of the physical reference desk. To be a good live virtual reference librarian, one must first be a good reference librarian. Core reference skills are the foundation for live virtual reference skills. Answering live virtual reference questions does differ enough from traditional desk reference, however, that specific training is required. Librarians will have to master real-time chat techniques and be deft at multitasking and manipulating open windows. They will have to be instructed in the procedures of specific live virtual reference software and informed of the library's live virtual reference policies. The amount of training each individual librarian receives will vary depending on the individual librarian's skills, and the model of live virtual reference the library has chosen.

REFERENCES

Read, Brendan B. 2001. "Readying Your Front Lines for Battle." *Call Center Magazine* (October): 44–54.

Sauers, Michael P. 2001. *Using the Internet as a Reference Tool : A How-To-Do-It Manual for Librarians*. New York: Neal-Schuman.

Throne, Adam. 2001. "The Training Game." *Call Center Magazine* (March): 44–57.

9 MARKETING FOR LIVE VIRTUAL REFERENCE

After training, you are ready to launch your service and begin marketing it. Marketing means getting the word out about your new live virtual reference service—what it is and what it can do for your patrons. In the past, marketing library services was thought to be either unnecessary or unwanted. Unnecessary because libraries for a long time had a near monopoly on the sources of information. If you wanted to do research, you had to pay a visit to the physical library. Case closed. There was no need for librarians to do any marketing. Marketing library services has long been unwanted because libraries are nonprofit organizations. Marketing is a set of for-profit techniques designed to get more people using your product. In the corporate world, if more people use a company's product, this can mean additional compensation for employees or increased staff to deal with heavier workloads. More people using reference services, however, can ultimately lead to burnout for reference librarians, and poorer service for patrons.

Recently, both of these reasons for avoiding marketing have been undermined. The arrival of the Internet means that libraries and librarians no longer have a monopoly on the sources of information for research. One library survey indicated that only about a third of users thought of the library first when seeking information (Shankman, 2001). What was in first place? If you said search engines, you'd be right. People are asking Ask Jeeves two million questions a day (Coffman and McGlamery, 2000). WebHelp, a question and answer service originally intended to be used internally in large corporations, was clocking hundreds of thousands of visitors a day before they limited access to the service (Lewis, 2001). The millions of people now searching for all sorts of information on the Web often don't think to look on library Web pages, but they do know all about Yahoo and Google and AskJeeves.

Most users don't even think about coming to a librarian for help when they believe information can be found online (Shankman, 2001). Librarians are just not on the radar screens of most people. Try it out. Ask some acquaintance or relative if they have ever called a librarian when they had a question or information need. Not when they wanted a book but when they wanted to know something that a librarian could help them find out. But, you say, we get lots of questions at our reference desk.

That may be true, but it's still only a tiny percentage of your user population. We now operate in a competitive environment. We can't go on assuming that patrons will continue to come to us because they always have in the past. We need to offer a better service and make sure people are aware of it.

Second, in many libraries burnout for reference librarians is no longer the problem; declining questions is. The number of questions asked and answered at physical reference desks have been going down since the advent of the Internet. This is one of the motivations for doing virtual reference in the first place—to make it easier for users to ask questions. Most chat reference services, however, receive only a handful of questions, following the general pattern of e-mail reference. When e-mail reference first began, many librarians expressed concern that they'd be overwhelmed with questions and they wouldn't be able to handle the demand. This didn't happen. In most cases, libraries discovered that they could fairly easily handle the new e-mail service, even though staff spent considerably more time on the typical e-mail question than on the average in-person question. The e-mail service could be managed and integrated into the workflow fairly smoothly, because there just weren't that many questions.

The outcome has been similar for some live virtual reference services, but there are some encouraging signs. The University of Illinois at Urbana-Champaign (UIUC) reported about 150 questions a week during October of 2001 (Wei Ma, 2002). Wesleyan University, a small liberal arts school with less than three thousand students, reported about 75 questions a week during a busy period in the fall of 2001, and they had only been offering the service a short time (Alan Hayard, 2001).

Still the fact remains that chat reference usage statistics aren't knocking anybody's socks off. Stephen Francoeur, creator of the *The Teaching Librarian* Web site, offers a theory for the paucity of response to live ref services. He suggests that users don't associate chat itself with a way of getting help for anything. They use it for instant messaging between friends and family, chatting with a celebrity online, or chatting in a chat room devoted to a commonly held interest (Francouer, 2001).

Transaction numbers are low for chat reference services for a combination of reasons: libraries often don't get the word out, live reference is a new service, people don't expect to use chat for asking informational and research questions, and some libraries have intentionally kept the service low key.

Bernie Sloan, a leading digital reference researcher, in a discussion about the relatively low numbers of live reference questions coming in to libraries so far, stressed the importance of marketing and emphasized that we need to discover and create new ways to let people know what we're doing (Sloan, 2001). Our challenge is not simply to make people aware that we offer a new information service at our library or a new access point, but to educate the general public (and our specific constituencies) about what exactly it is that reference librarians do. Providing and marketing live virtual reference services is a giant step in that direction.

People have certainly thought about library marketing before. Quite a number of books and articles about marketing your library have been written. One of the major points to be made about marketing is that it is more than promotion, publicity, or advertising. Marketing is a broad concept, with a number of facets. Philip Kotler created a model he called "the 4 P's." Kotler's model took successful private sector marketing strategies and adapted them to the nonprofit sector (Kotler, 1982). Weingand adapted and defined these 4 P's for the library profession. They include:

> Product: Those programs and services that the library provides to its customers.
> Price: What it costs to produce its product, plus any user fees that are assessed.
> Place: How products and customers (or patrons) are connected; distribution channels.
> Promotion: How the library communicates with its customers, relating details on how customer needs have been identified and what responses have been developed to meet those needs (Weingand, 1998).

For live virtual reference, the product is the online help service provided. The price includes not only the cost of the software but also staff time spent developing, implementing, and operating the service. You should also factor in any hardware and software used, but only that portion that would not have been used anyway. For example, the computer on your reference desk and the computer on your desk are used for many other things and would have been there regardless. But if you purchase or dedicate a computer to be used specifically for live reference or buy software such as EZProxy to authenticate users, then those costs should be included. The place (distribution channel) in this context would be the computer networks that transmit data. Promotion includes all the ways the library makes known its live reference service to patrons.

Do you recall our discussion of planning from Chapter 4? We

recommended that you survey your external and internal environments. One approach to beginning a marketing effort is to use a method that merges the planning and marketing processes. The first step is to do a marketing audit, which combines an analysis of the library's external environment and an assessment of the library's strengths and limitations (internal environment) (Weingand, 1998).

After that assessment is done, you should next work through the 4 P's listed above and consider how they can be defined for your specific situation. Finally, you need to undertake an evaluation to determine which aspects of your plan were effective and which ones weren't. We'll discuss evaluation in more depth in a later chapter.

Librarians are not salespeople, and for many going out and beating the bushes for business doesn't come naturally. But the skills and techniques necessary to market your library can be learned. And you'll find that many of the things you're already doing, like building relationships with various groups in your community or institution form the foundation of any marketing plan. You've been constructing this foundation and laying the groundwork over the years with all the community programs you've provided and all the services and materials you've made available to your patrons. We'll now discuss marketing live virtual reference within the context of the five models.

MARKETING THE BASIC MODEL

Now that we've discussed the importance of marketing, we're going to explain how it can be done on a modest scale. The basic model uses the "put up a link and they will come" marketing plan. Very little in the way of promotion or advertising is necessary. You have a limited budget, limited staff, and you're experimenting. You of course hope some people will try out the service, but you don't really want hordes, because you're not at that stage yet. The basic model is built on the notion of getting a service up and running quickly and one aspect you can easily limit is the time spent developing a marketing plan. With "keep it simple" as your motto, there are a few easy things you can do to alert your patrons that you're offering a new service (see page 135).

Use your established channels of communication. The basic model allows you to "get going" without getting bogged down in lots of analysis and committee meetings and wrangling about

Marketing for the Basic Model

1. Put a link on your homepage. The link should be on the library homepage, not buried two or three levels down. Real estate on the homepage itself may be scarce, but placing a button there greatly increases the chance of someone using the service.

   If you want to maximize potential usage, it's worth doing whatever politicking is necessary to get your piece of the page. On the other hand, if you really want to limit usage, you can place the icon deeper in the site and if it turns out that no one comes, you can always move it up to a more prominent spot. The design and placement of this link are very important.

2. Put a link in the new services and resources section. This section probably already exists on your library Web site, so just make sure you have a link there. A "new" icon of some sort is good, too, but no blinking lightbulbs or flashing colors, ok?

3. Create a distinctive icon or button that will catch the user's eye and be memorable. This may not be so simple, but it's worth it to develop a distinctive logo and a "brand identity" for your chat reference.

   (This should be considered optional, since it may take more time and energy than you want to devote to it if you're sticking with a basic model.)

4. Put a link to live reference on every page of your Web site and online catalog. Every Web page may not be feasible, but you want to have a link on as many pages as possible. This costs you nothing except time and is something that is recommended by many of the most experienced pioneers in the field, including Joe Janes (VRD Conference, 2000) and Steve Coffman (ACRL-DVC conference, 2001). Wesleyan University, as mentioned previously, was receiving 75 questions a week after only being operational for two months and they attributed much of their chat reference's popularity to the decision to put a link on as many pages as they could.

5. Mention your new service in the library newsletter. If you have a newsletter, online or in print, make sure there is an announcement in it giving details and encouraging people to try it out and give you feedback.

6. Create a flyer/handout/brochure that can be distributed from the reference desk or classroom or speaking engagement. These flyers can easily be given to patrons who come to the desk and provide a way to lead into a brief description of chat reference. These materials have also been used to good effect by many libraries, such as Q and A NJ and MIT.

7. Encourage librarians to mention your live reference service during their regular contact with patrons. This might be during story hours, library instruction sessions, an orientation, or a community program.

"what if's?" You've decided chat reference has potential and you want to move ahead and get your feet wet. After you have some experience under your belt, you can decide if you wish to invest more energy and resources and develop a full-blown marketing plan for the service.

MARKETING THE HOMEGROWN MODEL

The homegrown or open source model shares many similarities with the basic model. The major difference is that the software used is not a commercially available product, but one that has been created at your institution or through an open source project. At Temple, after our initial experience with a commercial software package called TalkBack, we ended up developing our own software—Temple TalkNow.

We had some idea of what to expect when we switched to our homegrown software, since we had been doing chat reference for about a year. We had demonstrated that students were willing to ask questions using chat. We had one link on the homepage, but a user had to scroll down to see it. We had another link one level down, reached by clicking our large "ask us!" text on the homepage. We continued to send out e-mail notifying various university departments and some additional announcements appeared in newsletters, but we remained low key for the most part. Staff shortages precluded us from taking any steps to really ramp up and expand the service.

A few other librarians outside of Temple were aware of our project since we had posted questions to listservs and we were invited to speak at a local library conference in the spring of 1999, which helped to spread the word in the library community. Subsequent conference presentations and articles raised our profile and other librarians began to ask for copies of the TalkNow software to try out.

From a marketing perspective, one unique aspect of the homegrown model is that you'll be marketing your software to other institutions if you follow the open source approach. The open source concept is to make the software you've created easily available to others so that they can use, modify, and enhance it. The person who downloads the software modifies and improves it and the enhanced version of your software is then again made available to all comers in a continuing cycle that works to the mutual benefit of everyone. Here are some techniques you can use to make the larger library community aware of your live reference software.

> **Ways to Distribute and Publicize Your Homegrown Software**
>
> - Create a Web site to keep people up-to-date about your project and let everyone download from there.
> - Present at conferences, describing your experience and your software.
> - Write journal articles.
> - Post messages to listservs and discussion groups.
> - Convey targeted messages to specific individuals at other libraries using e-mail, the telephone, and face-to-face contact.
> - Post your software on the oss4lib Web site (open source systems for libraries).

MARKETING THE ADVANCED MODEL

You've decided to go beyond the experimental or demonstration stage and are ready to commit significant resources to your live reference project. Since you're sinking a lot of time and energy into this new service, one area you don't want to neglect is marketing. If you have administrators who are weighing the time and resources being devoted to live virtual reference against the relative number of people served, you will need to put some of these marketing strategies in place to improve your ratios. Your users need to know this new online reference help service exists and they need to know how it can help them.

Develop a marketing plan for your advanced model live virtual reference service. But how do you do that? The 4 P's model espoused by Kotler is a good starting point. The following quote from a paper by Aline Soules provides some additional insight. "At its most basic level, every member transaction, every interaction, every connection—positive or negative—is marketing. In a strategic context, marketing drives the entire decision-making process and requires research that is objective, comprehensive and continuous. Marketing is strategic on one hand, the responsibility of everyone on the other. It is a philosophy, not a job—a way of thinking, not a department" (Goldman, 1999). The plan you develop should be specific to your library. How do you define product, price, place (distribution), and promotion for your library and your community? One way to put more focus on the promotion component is to write these specific duties into someone's job description and then structure the job so that the person has time to devote to these activities. If such a position already exists in your library, work that into your live virtual reference marketing.

Another approach to library marketing is outsourcing. Although controversial, outsourcing can be effective. Outsourcing marketing activities to a company that employs experts to develop and implement a marketing plan worked well for the Cleveland Public Library (Virtual Reference Desk conference, 2001). The Peninsula, Silicon Valley, Bay Area, and County Library Systems also outsourced the design of their Web site to an outside agency. In addition, the agency created four-color oversized postcards that were sent out to all the residents of one of the cities (Henshall, 2001).

Libraries frequently offer terrific programs, services, and resources, but nobody knows about them. An example of this in both public and academic libraries is subscription databases. Libraries spend tens or even hundreds of thousands of dollars for these fabulous research tools and often only a very small percentage of the clientele even know they exist. How many times have you spoken to a user who needed an article from a popular magazine or journal or a description found in an encyclopedia who had no idea it was available online from the local public library? Getting the word out must become a much higher priority.

One innovative approach is the e-branch library created by Public Information Kiosk, Inc. This product combines phone lines and fax machines with touch screens, computers, and internet access. The e-branch is helping to expand library service to low-income, rural, and under-served areas and to nontraditional locations. (Grenier, 2001). An example is the e-branch with customized homework-helper Web links set up by the Platteville, Colorado, Public Library in the cafeteria of a high school in Gilcrest, a town of about 1,000. In Maryland, the Enoch Pratt Free Library kiosk in a Safeway grocery store allows University of Maryland students to check their e-mail (Grenier, 2001).

One of the best ways to communicate the existence and usefulness of your live reference service is to develop partnerships with other groups on campus, in your city or county or within your institution. These groups have information needs that you can help with and constituencies they can notify about your service. These could be academic computer services, the office of online learning, or another city government department. Start thinking about the groups you work with and ask them if you can put a link on their Web page. Here are some other ways to market your advanced model live virtual reference service.

> **Marketing for the Advanced Model**
>
> 1. Putting links inside the research databases themselves. This is possible with some databases already, and libraries need to work with and encourage more vendors to follow suit.
> 2. The icon itself should be memorable, something catchy that makes an impression and sticks in the user's mind. Perhaps your library or institution has a logo that can be made into an icon or button. The placement of the icon on the page is also important. It needs to be positioned so that it's easily seen and clearly obvious, yet doesn't distract from the main focus of the page. This is an objective that is not always easily achieved, which is the reason we now have people who make their living as Web designers.
> 3. You should also try to get your live ref link placed on the pages of other departments within your organization. Developing partnerships with other departments can be helpful because they can promote your service when talking to their constituencies and going about their daily business.
> 4. If you provide in-person or online orientations for patrons, be sure to mention the live reference service. Whenever you offer user education or orientation classes or do presentations for a group in the library or in the community, use the opportunity to highlight live reference.
> 5. Newspaper and magazine articles can be exceptionally effective and reach large numbers of people. An excellent example of this is the phenomenal impact of a single newspaper article. When the CLEVNET consortium launched their new live service, they sent out notices to many media outlets. Only one reporter showed up. However, that one reporter happened to be from the Cleveland Plain Dealer. The paper ran the story and it was picked up by AP, CNN, NPR, and others (VRD 2001, presentation). This is an example of a real success story that demonstrates what's possible.
> 6. Remember your local radio and tv stations too. A lot of people listen to these stations and it's a way to potentially connect with a whole new constituency.
> 7. Don't forget word of mouth, sometimes the most powerful of all. One person uses your chat reference, has a good experience and tells his friends, who are willing to give it a try because it's been recommended. They trust their friend's judgment.

MARKETING THE COLLABORATIVE MODEL

A live virtual reference service being provided by a consortium is likely to have greater combined resources to bring to bear on a marketing effort. You have a much larger pool of librarians from whom creative ideas can be gleaned. But along with those greater resources comes greater complexity. You have many different libraries that will have to meet and agree on all the components of developing and maintaining a service. Political issues will surface regarding who's responsbile for what, who's actually doing what, and who pays for what. You will probably have a project manager for each individual library and a project manager for the entire consortium. Working out the structure of the collaborative arrangement itself can be time consuming.

In some collaborative arrangements, you'll be marketing your service to other libraries, much as we discussed marketing software in the homegrown model. The twist or unique aspect is that you'll be offering the opportunity to join an existing group and to participate in a complete service package, rather than simply a chance to use Open Source code in your own library any way you see fit. Sometimes all the members of a group will be included from the beginning, but often only a subset of the whole group will be involved at the start.

An example is the Q and A NJ project in New Jersey. Originally begun with 12 libraries, it now has about 25 libraries on board. Since the Q and A NJ project received startup money from a Library Services and Technology Act (LSTA) grant, it was in the enviable position of being able to invite other libraries in the consortium to join for free. When the barrier of spending hard dollars is removed, the other obstacles seem much less daunting.

The Metropolitan Cooperative Library System (MCLS) project in California started with a small subset of the total membership as well. The more active libraries often encourage the other libraries to get involved and participate. Sometimes it's a matter of size. The larger libraries have sufficient staff to take on a new project. A small library naturally finds it much more difficult to work out a way to join and participate in the new service while still maintaining all their existing services.

When inviting other libraries to participate, long-standing relationships and a comfort level developed by working with others in a consortium over a long period will help smooth the way and provide a climate conducive to experimentation.

Although you may end up being in a position to market to other libraries, your main focus will be on marketing to your patrons. The commercial media have been helpful to some library collaborative marketing efforts. A California consortium, for example, had help from the media in marketing their service. Articles appeared in local and regional newspapers about the Q & A Café in northern California. The Q & A Café also piloted their project in just two cities as a beginning step and then rolled it out to other cities. They authenticated users by zip code. A move to use library card numbers for authentication proved problematic

> **Marketing for the Collaborative Model**
>
> - Pool resources with other libraries
> - Avoid political conflicts
> - Use commercial media
> - Outsource to produce logos, bookmarks, fliers

because there were many different libraries in the consortium, all having different kinds of library cards. This is exactly the sort of problem that is likely to come up when you try to coordinate a service among individual libraries with established procedures.

Besides getting the word out to your local media, you may want to consider outsourcing parts of your marketing effort. The South Jersey Regional Library Cooperative contracted with a graphic designer to design logos, Web graphics, bookmarks, and posters for the group. The bookmarks and posters were distributed to all participating libraries.

The South Jersey Regional Library Cooperative (SJRLC) drafted a press release for Q and A NJ participating libraries. The libraries identified local newspapers and press releases were e-mailed and faxed to the papers. In addition, local Borders and Barnes and Noble bookstores agreed to distribute bookmarks. The SJRLC libraries will be reaching out to other local organizations to distribute flyers and bookmarks and put up Web links.

MARKETING THE CORPORATE MODEL

The final model is the corporate Web contact center. Investigating how large corporations see real-time customer service fitting into their overall marketing strategy can be instructive for libraries. Although there are certainly significant differences, there are also similarities. For-profit corporations have a very clear understanding of marketing and its crucial place in their operations. Marketing is defined by the American Marketing Association as: "...the process of planning and executing the conception, pricing, promotion, and distribution of ideas, goods, and services to create exchanges that satisfy individual and organizational objectives" Wenzel and Horowitz, 2001).

Business executives are interested in Web-based customer service or "electronic Customer Relationship Managment" (e-CRM) because it enhances the bottom line. According to one leading e-service software developer, "companies that don't develop effective e-service wind up spending far more on customer support than their competitors..." (Gianforte, 2001).

Customer Relationship Management (CRM), a term that you'll see frequently in the trade literature, refers not to software, but "to an organization's ability to improve the ways it communicates with customers based on information it continually gathers about them" (Fleischer, et al., 2001).

Some software now being used by libraries offers the ability to gather information about users. For instance, HumanClick Pro (humanclick.com), one of the most popular eCRM packages, offers a monitor tag feature that allows the agent to track a customer's progress around a Web site. This package also offers a repeat visitor identification feature that tells the librarian/agent if he's chatting with a returning customer and tells the agent which pages the customer has visited.

CRM is part of an overall marketing strategy and although companies are spending millions, they're discovering that implementing successful CRM programs is much more easily said than done. One report notes that successful CRM requires changing internal processes and procedures that are deeply entrenched (Fleischer, et al., 2001).

One popular service, WebHelp, offers real-time help to members for only $9.99/mo. Originally free, the service is now fee-based. You can get help from "web wizards" in real-time. The company also sells its software, so that other companies can set up their own live help centers [www.webhelp.com/home].

Web users want to find the information they need fast. They are very sensitive to delays and may only wait a few seconds before moving on if they don't get a response right away. The customer doesn't want to fill out an e-mail form and wait hours or days to get a response; they want it *now!* This puts a lot of pressure on not just Web site designers, but also on those who contribute to the content, which includes marketing and customer service staff, to anticipate the needs of a vast range of customers. In fact, they can't anticipate everyone's needs and that's where live customer service representatives come in. If the potential customer can speak to a company representative right away and explain what they need, the odds of making a sale increase significantly.

Libraries and reference librarians can learn a great deal from commercial organizations about marketing strategies. That knowledge can then be translated into reference settings and imbued

> **Marketing in the Corporate Model**
>
> 1. Pushing content. Businesses view this as a way to turn the customer's e-mail box into an extension of their Web site. They ask if you would like to be notified about changes, new products, and so on, and then "push" messages to you based on your request. Libraries have long had "current awareness" services and push technology can be used to provide such services.
>
> 2. Fast response. The user expects an answer now, not in a little while. This is a mantra. If the customer is disappointed once, they are likely to go elsewhere.
>
> 3. Track consistently. What questions are asked most frequently? Knowing the answer allows resources to be allotted more efficiently. This is more problematic for libraries than businesses since we get a wider variety of questions and more unique questions. However, in every library, certain questions recur over and over. Many live reference packages can help identify those questions and provide pre-scripted responses to save time.
>
> 4. Scalability. Businesses are focused on the need to be able to scale, so that volume doesn't exceed the company's ability to support increased communication.

with the values of librarianship that give our profession a global perspective and distinguish us from other information providers.

SUMMARY

Librarians haven't yet really figured out how to market live virtual reference services. Some initial attempts have been made, but most effort has gone into just getting a service off the ground. Efforts have been experimental, to see if it could be done, and if we did it, whether people would come. We did build it and people have started to come, but only in modest numbers.

The foundations of marketing for live virtual reference lie in activities that many libraries are already doing. Existing channels of communication, including library Web pages, newsletters, local and national media, word of mouth, flyers, and connections to other departments and organizations have been used to spread the word about our new services. These are all good and useful and necessary.

However, if live virtual reference is ever going to really take off and begin serving large numbers of users, we need to hone the tools we use to identify our users' needs and desires. Marketing is key. We need to focus significant resources on learning what early twenty-first-century users want from their library reference services and how to give it to them. We need to make libraries a service that people think of first, or at least in the same breath when they think of information providers.

REFERENCES

Coffman, Steve, and Susan McGlamery. 2000. "The Librarian and Mr. Jeeves." *American Libraries* (May 2000):31,5 p. 66–69.

Fleischer, Joe, Warren S. Hersch, and Lee Hollman. "Embodying CRM." *Call Center Magazine* (September, 2001):14,9.50–62.

Francouer, Stephen. DIG_REF June 4, 2001. Accessed 01/15/02.

Gianforte, Greg. "The Insider's Guide to Customer Service on the Web: Eight Secrets for Successful E-Service" [Online]. Available: www.rightnow.com/resource/whitepaper.html [2001, February 11].

Goldman, Neil. 1999. "All for One Survival Marketing." *Credit Union Management* (November): 46.

Grenier, Melinda Patterson. 2001. "PIK Stands on Its '24/7' e-Branch Library." *Wall Street Journal* Eastern Edition (July 12): 10.

Hayard, Alan. DIG_REF 12/10/01. Accessed 1/19/02.

Henshall, Kay. DIG_REF 3/8/01. Accessed 1/20/02.

Kotler, Philip. 1982. *Marketing for Non-Profit Organizations*. Englewood Cliffs, N.J.: Prentice-Hall.

Lewis, Michael. 2001. "Faking It." *New York Times Magazine* (July 15).

Ma, Wei. DIG_REF 1/16/02. Accessed 1/17/02.

Shankman, Larry. DIG_REF 12/06/01. Accessed 1/15/02.

Sloan, Bernie. DIG_REF 06/19/01. Accessed 1/15/2002.

Weingand, Darlene E. 1998. *Future Driven Library Marketing*. Chicago: American Library Association.

Wenzel, Sarah G., and Lisa Horowitz. 2001. Marketing Virtual Reference: Is Discretion Still the Better Part of Valor? Presentation at Virtual Reference Desk conference, Nov. 12, 2001.

10 EVALUATING YOUR LIVE VIRTUAL REFERENCE

Just as evaluation of reference services by ongoing review and assessment is important for face-to-face reference, so is it important for virtual reference. Evaluating a *live* virtual reference service is of special concern since it is a new service. New software, new models of staffing, new techniques for answering questions, a new vision of what reference is. Fortunately, we can ground our practice of evaluating live virtual reference in the same principles and methods used to evaluate face-to-face reference (Whitlatch, 2001).

One difference, however, is the amount of data on patron-librarian interactions that can be retrieved from many live virtual reference software packages. Another is that since live virtual reference may be a pilot project for your library, you can ask the question: should we continue to offer this service? If so, what can we change to make it better? Frankly, the verdict is not yet in on how effective live virtual reference is as a way of mediating between patrons and information. Is the amount of work you are doing worth the time and effort you are putting into it? What is the right mix of face-to-face, Web page FAQs, e-mail virtual reference, and live virtual reference? We are in the process of finding out, and assessment is important for all of us. In this chapter, we outline a process that can be used for evaluating all the models, then discuss each model individually.

PROCESS FOR EVALUATING ALL MODELS

The process for evaluating live virtual reference can be broken down into these steps:

- Revisit Your Vision
- Evaluate Software
- Assess Staffing
- Review Questions
- Analyze Answers
- Produce a Report

Revisit Your Vision
• What is the most important reason you are offering live virtual reference? • Set a standard for evaluation.

REVISIT YOUR VISION

The process of evaluation should begin with revisiting your vision and your reasons for starting a live virtual reference service. Remember again why are you doing this in the first place. Is it to bring new patrons to the library? To serve distance learners? To reach users where they are? To be on the cutting edge? To not get left behind? To provide another way for your patrons to ask questions? To develop your librarians' digital skills? To collaborate with colleagues? To try something new? All of the above? You may have multiple reasons for doing live virtual reference and you may wish to fulfill more than one objective by doing it. But try to think of the most important reason, because this should influence what and how you evaluate. For example, if your main objective is to serve distance learners, then the question of whether in-person reference is "better" than live virtual reference is either irrelevant or misguided. If your main objective is to develop librarian skills, then as long as your librarians are answering questions, your service should continue to operate. Be clear on what you are evaluating and why. Then set a performance standard for what constitutes success in the area in which you want to evaluate.

EVALUATE SOFTWARE

If your software isn't functioning properly, you can't have a live virtual reference service. On the most rudimentary level, you have to evaluate if the software is working at all. That is, are questions coming in and are reference librarians able to answer them in real-time? This may sound simple, but it does require that someone (the project manager or systems librarian for example) pay attention to it. A physical reference desk shouldn't have too many technical problems that you need to worry about (is the desk there? can people walk up to it?). A live virtual reference service point, on the other hand, needs to be checked on a daily basis or any time a problem comes up. If everything is working ok, you're fine. But if a problem occurs, you need to troubleshoot and identify the cause of the problem. You have to figure out if the problem is with the software, or if it is a human problem. If it is a

> **Evaluate Software Checklist**
>
> - Is it working at all?
> - Can you fix or troubleshoot?
> - How well are the features working?
> - Is the software messing up your hardware?
> - Ask reference librarians for suggestions for improvement.

problem with the software, is it on the user side or on the librarian side? If you have the know-how, you can fix it, but if not you may have to spend some time (maybe a long time) talking to the technical support services of your software vendor. If they have tech support. If the problem is serious enough, you may have to shut your service down for a few days or even indefinitely.

Also evaluate how well the features of the software are working. Is chat working correctly? Is it slow? Is there anything wrong with it? For example, in chat your librarians must be able to see a running script of the entire conversation. If not it can be very hard to carry on a conversation. Are you actually able to push Web pages to patrons? Are you able to negotiate frames with patrons? Are patrons getting disconnected? Why?

Consider what the software is doing to your hardware. Is it creating lots of temporary files that are hogging memory and making your machine run slower? You can answer most of these questions by asking your reference librarians for their feedback, informally at the reference desk or during weekly meetings. Ask them what features of the software they think could be improved upon.

ASSESS STAFFING

Are you able to staff the service? That is, are people at least showing up, so to speak? If you staff your service from your reference desk, you are at least guaranteed that when the reference desk is staffed there should be someone available to answer live reference questions. But are they really? Or are they away from the reference computer, helping patrons away from the desk? Are they ignoring live questions when they come in by shunting them to e-mail? How does the staff feel about the service? Are they enthusiastic or are they grumbling about it behind the project coordinator's back? Identify the librarians who are having problems. If possible, ask the more proficient librarians to serve as mentors. If some librarians are just beyond hope consider going to a volunteer staffing arrangement. Some casual observation,

Assess Staffing Checklist
• Are staff available to answer questions? • Are they enthusiastic or disparaging? • Should you go to a volunteer staffing arrangment?

gentle probing, or direct questioning of your staff can reveal how staff are responding to live virtual reference.

REVIEW QUESTIONS

One of the most popular ways to evaluate live virtual reference is to count the number of questions you are receiving. Determine how many questions are coming in and compare this number at least to your e-mail reference questions and if possible to your in-person questions as well. Do this in the least labor intensive way. Although it may be easy to see how many questions are coming in on a weekly, daily, or even hourly basis, for someone to look at this data and make sense of it is something else. Set up a spreadsheet and fit it into the project manager or head of reference's workflow.

Simply counting questions is not enough. You must *evaluate*. How many questions constitutes success in meeting your mission? In some models, a low number of questions may not be so bad. As long as you are helping a few patrons a day in real-time and developing your live virtual reference skills, that may be enough, especially in the first six months to one year of your service. Don't expect patrons to all of a sudden start asking all their questions virtually, and don't think live virtual reference is a failure if you don't completely replace the physical reference desk immediately. There is a tendency to think that if e-mail or face-to-face reference receives many more questions than live virtual reference, then live virtual reference is not worth doing at all. Give the new service a chance. And give your patrons some time to get used to asking questions in a new way. On the other hand, if you are receiving more questions than you can handle, then you should start to think about how to limit the service or upgrading to a more advanced software and staffing model. At this point, you could also start thinking about quantity of questions in terms of peak and downtime hours. Are there hours when traffic is heavy or light? Decide if you want to continue with your current hours, expand the hours, or limit the hours.

In addition to quantifying the number of questions, look at the types of questions you are receiving and who is asking them. Are

Review Questions Checklist
• How many questions are you receiving? • How many questions constitutes success? • What time of day or day of the week has the most questions? The least? • What kinds of questions are you receiving? • Who's asking the questions?

there certain kinds of questions, ready-reference for example, that are outnumbering other questions? Can you turn some of these questions into frequently asked question lists? Are certain kinds of questions easier for your librarians to answer in this format than others? Can you identify who your users are—by geographic location, age level, or class level? Are these the users you intended to reach when you started the service?

ANALYZE ANSWERS

If your software keeps transcripts of live virtual reference sessions, you can evaluate the quality of librarian answers and measure user satisfaction. By analyzing transcripts, you can determine if librarians are following the techniques for effective live chat—using short messages, typing grammatical sentences with a minimum of typing errors, being friendly and informal, not being rude, using scripted messages, multitasking, and giving factually correct and complete information. Unfortunately evaluating transcripts, although sometimes fascinating reading, is time consuming. Try to glance at the transcripts at least once a week and look for warning signs: questions that are not being answered, a pattern of incomplete answers, unhappy patron responses. Deal with these issues as they come up, one-on-one with the librarian or in general at a reference staff meeting.

Check to see that the agreed upon live virtual reference policies are being followed. This is a good time to revisit your privacy policy. In analyzing answers, privacy is important for both the user and the answering librarian. If you are maintaining an archive of questions and answers, strip out the user's identifying information. If you are using some answers for training purposes, strip out the librarian's identifying information as well. Having answers evaluated makes many librarians nervous. Deal with a librarian whose answers could use improvement, either in terms of core reference skills or chat techniques, but do so in a way that is sensitive to that person's professionalism.

By analyzing answers you can also attempt to gauge user satis-

> **Analyze Answers Checklist**
>
> - Are librarians following techniques for real-time chat?
> - Are all questions being answered thoroughly?
> - Are live virtual reference policies being followed?
> - Is patron response positive or negative?

faction. Look for user comments. Are there a lot of the "this is a great service!" variety? Or are a lot of users tersely disconnecting? To be more scientific, you could have a brief survey on your Web site asking users to rate their live reference encounter and make any comments or suggestions. An example of such a survey is the one at the University of Illinois at Urbana-Champaign (Kibbee, et al., 2002)

PRODUCE A REPORT

Produce a written report of your evaluation so as to have documentation of where you are with your live virtual reference service at a certain date. Create your own format, or follow the format here. Include a written narrative and any statistics you can generate about the number of questions or comments that reveal user satisfaction. At the end of the report, include a conclusion that states how well the service is matching your original vision, whether or not you will continue the service, and what can be changed about the service. If any interesting insights come out of your report, consider publishing an article about your service. You will be contributing to a growing best practices literature. For an excellent example of a published report see "Virtual Service, Real Data: Results of a Pilot Study" (Kibbee, et al., 2002).

We have just covered the process of evaluating live virtual reference as it applies to all five models of live virtual reference. Now it's time to look more closely at how these areas can be applied specifically to the five models.

EVALUATING THE BASIC MODEL

Although most of us agree on the importance of evaluation and assessment—let's be honest—not all of us have the time to do it or the means to do it they way we'd like. The practitioner of the basic model always asks, what's the least I have to do? A minimalist approach to evaluation involves setting up the service,

Worksheet for an Evaluation Report

Date:

Vision

The reason why we are offering live virtual reference is _____ .

Software

The software we are using is _____ .

The software is/is not satisfactory because _____ .

Staffing

The staffing model we are using is _____ .

The staffing is/is not satisfactory because _____ .

Questions

The number of questions we have received is _____ .

Most questions are received during the hours of _____ on _____ day of the week.

The questions we are receiving fall into the following categories _____ .

The questions are being asked by _____ .

We are happy/unhappy with how many questions we have received and who is asking them.

Answers

Librarians are/are not following techniques for real-time chat.

Questions are/are not being answered thoroughly.

Live virtual reference policies are/are not being followed.

Patron response has been mostly positive/negative. Some examples include _____ .

Conclusion

The first _____ months of the live virtual reference project was a success/needs improvement.

We will continue with live virtual reference but will make the following changes

_____ .

making sure it's working, and then trying not to pay too much attention to it. Many physical reference desks operate in this way—as long as the building is open and a librarian is staffing the desk, many reference librarians don't do much evaluation. Statistics may be collected. A librarian may be gently advised on an answer to a patron or frequently asked questions may be discussed in a weekly reference meeting. The guiding principle behind basic live virtual reference service is to fit it into your existing reference scheme without too much disruption. So at minimum, the corresponding task to seeing that the building is open is seeing that the virtual reference software is working correctly. Corresponding to ensuring that a librarian is staffing the desk is ensuring that a librarian is staffing the virtual desk. Just as you count the number of physical desk questions and judge the quality of librarian answers, so too will you count the number of live virtual questions and judge the quality of virtual answers. Some software that is suggested for the basic model, AOL Instant Messenger for example, does not provide a way to archive questions and answers, making detailed data collection and analysis impossible. Which is really a blessing in disguise. The basic model is all about simplicity—simple model, simple evaluation.

EVALUATING THE HOMEGROWN MODEL

As in training and marketing, evaluating in the homegrown model is similar to the basic model. Since the software is not expensive, extensive evaluation may be less of a priority. But if you've invested a lot of time into creating and maintaining your open source code, evaluation may take on more importance. You can go into as much depth as you like in the evaluation, but special attention should be paid to the open source aspects of software.

Ensure that the software is working correctly, the librarians know how to use it, and whether or not any features could be improved. Since you have created the code, you have an opportunity to make it work the way you want to. The ability to communicate with the authors of your source code is essential. If the authors of your code create your software and then go off to work on other projects, you won't be able to make any improvements or fix bugs.

Another element of the homegrown or open source model is

making your software available so that other libraries can use it for free and make improvements on it. The most difficult part of being part of an open source project is trying to make the software as user-friendly as possible for other libraries. Evaluate how easily other libraries can download it and use it. If more libraries are downloading it and using it, the more chance there is that they will improve upon it. Evaluate how well you have promoted your open source software. You can stir up interest in your product, your library, and the open source movement by making presentations at library conferences. Create a clear Web page where other libraries can download your software as painlessly as possible. For a good example of homegrown software that is easy to download, see Rakim from Miami University (Ohio) available for download at styro.lib.muohio.edu/rakim/.

EVALUATING THE ADVANCED MODEL

Evaluation takes on more importance in the advanced model. Since you are paying more money for the software and its features, putting a lot of time into training, creating another reference schedule and adding to your librarians' reference hours, you really want to make sure that what you are doing is worth the time and money you are putting into it. This means spending even more time on evaluation. The four categories of evaluation remain the same—software, staffing, questions, and answers—but everything is treated more thoroughly and in a more formal manner by more detailed reporting and analyzing transcripts more closely.

SOFTWARE

Since your software costs more money, you definitely want to see that it is working every day and not malfunctioning. Keep a log of any technical failures, how soon they were fixed, quality of the customer service you received, and the time you spent resolving the issue. If you have recurrent problems with an aspect of your software or receive poor customer service it may be time to look for new software. More importantly, you want to be able to evaluate how well your librarians are using all the advanced features you are paying for. Are you paying for features that are not being used and perhaps are not needed? Are there some features that you want that you can ask the vendor to develop more fully.

STAFFING

In addition to the staffing evaluation performed in the basic model, you have to judge whether or not the complicated scheduling you are doing is working. Are reference librarians showing up for their allotted hours? Are they happy or unhappy about it? Is their other work suffering? You can take a more formal approach by interviewing reference librarians for their reaction to the service on a regular basis. If you have librarians who are unhappy about live virtual reference, listen to what they don't like about it. If you have librarians who are incapable of being reformed, it might be time to go to a volunteer staffing model.

QUESTIONS

An advanced model of evaluation will involve close inspection of the mass of detailed usage statistics supplied by most sophisticated software packages. It will be up to you to wade through this data and make sense of it. Since all calls are recorded, you can keep a detailed tally of the number of questions received and answered down to the hour. If you can determine what hours are the busiest and which are the slowest, you can begin to decide how to allocate your staff time more efficiently.

So that you are not simply looking at numbers for the sake of looking at numbers, devise some benchmarks of comparison. As in the basic model, compare the number of live virtual reference questions to the number of e-mail and in-person questions. Chart your progress over time. The number of live virtual reference questions you are getting should be growing. A simple method of comparison is to note for the same unit of time (week or month) the percentage of live reference questions received compared to e-mail and in-person questions. Three benchmarks to use are 50 percent, 100 percent and 150 percent. If the number of live virtual reference questions reaches 50 percent of in-person questions, for example, you could begin to form a justification for halving your desk staffing and assigning the other half to answer live reference questions exclusively. The other important number here is the number of in-person questions over time. If that number is declining while live virtual reference is rising, it could be that your in-person users are moving to the Web. However, if your in-person questions stay the same, but live virtual reference questions rise, then you can hypothesize that you are reaching new users. It's also possible to experience the virtual reference paradox: live virtual reference actually increases your in-person numbers. By connecting with a patron online, you have made the person aware of the services available at the library.

ANSWERS

Written transcripts of live virtual reference sessions are provided with advanced virtual reference software. In general, this is new for us. We've never really had automatic, complete transcripts of our work before. At the face-to-face physical reference desk, it is of course possible in theory to write down questions and answers or audio tape and transcribe them, but that is extremely labor intensive. Now that we have an instant record of live reference transactions we must decide what to do with this mountain of data.

Analyzing transcripts is actually a tremendous opportunity to become informed about patron needs and to use the knowledge to improve services. But first things first: make sure your users are protected by a clear privacy policy. If you use any data you have collected in a public way get written permission or strip out any identifying information including names, e-mail addresses, and place names. Also be sure to protect the privacy of your librarians.

One way to attempt to get the most out of the live virtual reference transcripts is to create a database of answers, sometimes called a knowledge base. A knowledge base holds out the promise of being a searchable record of reference work, so that repeat questions can be answered from the knowledge base. As was said previously, since libraries receive such a broad array of questions, it is not clear how useful such knowledge bases are. One problem is that instead of saving work, the knowledge base must be maintained, which creates more work. For an example of a library knowledge base see the Keystone Library Network's Virtual Information Desk at libweb.mnsfld.edu/vid/vid-kb.asp.

EVALUATING THE COLLABORATIVE MODEL

All of the evaluation issues previously discussed apply to the collaborative model as well, with one important difference. In the collaborative model, different libraries join together to answer reference questions. To ensure uniformity and quality control of answers, consortium participants should work toward outlining common standards that they all can agree to. An important effort toward achieving this goal has been initiated by the Virtual Reference Desk AskA Consortium (Kasowitz, et al., 2000). Although the standards outlined are intended for AskA services, they can also be applied to other forms of virtual reference, such as live virtual reference. (For a more recent effort of standards see McClure, et al., 2002.) Progress has also been made in the area of common standards by the Library of Congress Collaborative Digital Reference Service (CDRS). For the most recent update of their activity see lcweb.loc.gov/rr/digiref/.

EVALUATING THE CORPORATE MODEL

Like the corporate staffing model, evaluation in the corporate model is best seen as a model to be avoided. In the corporate model, low-paid workers are expected to follow a strict script in giving answers and are reprimanded when they deviate from the script (Dilevko, 2001). Electronic surveillance is used to monitor phone calls, e-mails, and text chat for quality assurance. Even screen captures are used to monitor what Web pages are sent to customers (Fleischer, 2001). Formulas called metrics are used to quantify and measure everything from how long an operator should spend with a customer to how long customers will tolerate being on hold (Jackson, 2002; Fluss, 2001). Consultants may be brought in to evaluate the efficiency of the call center (Hollman, 2001). In economic downtimes call centers will be evaluated on their ROI—return on investment. If call centers can't show that they are reducing costs and increasing profits they are often eliminated (Fluss, 2001). Corporate call centers are known for their high turnover of staff. We can't imagine many librarians who would want to work in these conditions. Instead of moving forward into the digital age, corporate call centers seem to be going backward to the sweatshop. Does a digital model of service entail that libraries must adopt these Taylorist techniques? We believe the answer is no. Again, libraries can fall back on traditional library models of evaluation that are better suited to providing service in a nonprofit environment. Beware of the corporate model of evaluation when evaluating your live virtual reference service.

SUMMARY

Live virtual reference is an experiment. Evaluation is the way you learn what is working and what isn't. Now is the time to step back from the project and reflect on how well it's meeting its mission. Here's your chance to fix what you don't like. In a way, you are really going back to step one of the planning process to decide what can be tweaked or changed. Although there are a lot of new aspects to live virtual reference, it is really an evolution from traditional face-to-face reference, not a revolution. Technology changes, but our mission to connect users with information remains constant. Let your service continue to evolve. Re-envision your mission. Get new committee members. Change your service model by joining a consortium or getting new software. Refine your policies. Publish your results and learn from your colleagues. Through purposeful experimentation with technology and careful evaluation of service models, we can ensure the survival of reference service without betraying our traditional reference values.

REFERENCES

Dilevko, Juris. 2001. "An Ideological Analysis of Digital Reference Service Models." *Library Trends* 50, no. 2 (Fall): 218–244.

Fleischer, Joe. 2001. "The Whole Story." *Call Center Magazine* 14, no. 11 (November): 32–43.

Fluss, Donna. 2001. "Playing and Winning the Numbers Game." *Call Center Magazine* 14, no. 11 (November): 14–28.

Hollman, Lee. 2001. "Steer Your Call Center Toward Greater Efficiency." *Call Center Magazine* 14, no. 15 (May): 40–52.

Jackson, Kathryn. 2002. "Thinking Beyond the Old 80/20 Rule." *Call Center Magazine* 15, no. 1 (January): 54–67.

Kasowitz, Abby, Blythe Bennett, and R. David Lankes. 2000. "Quality Standards for Digital Reference Consortia." *Reference and User Services Quarterly* 39, no. 4: 355–363.

Kibbee, Jo, David Ward, and Wei Ma. 2002. "Virtual Service, Real Data: Results of a Pilot Study." *Reference Services Review* 30, no. 1: 25–36.

McClure, Charles R., R. David Lankes, Melissa Gross, and Beverly Choltco-Devlin. *Statistics, Measures, and Quality Standards for Assessing Digital Reference Library Services: Guidelines and Procedures Field Test Draft: March 8, 2002* [Online]. Available: quartz.syr.edu/quality/Field_ Test_ Draft.pdf [2002, April 29].

Whitlatch, Jo Bell. 2001. "Evaluating Reference Services in the Electronic Age." *Library Trends* 50, no. 2, (Fall): 207–217.

GLOSSARY

24/7—reference services that operate 24 hours a day, seven days a week. Also the name of a live virtual reference software vendor.

asynchronous—not in real-time. A characteristic of e-mail virtual reference.

audio cue—a sound that alerts you when a live virtual reference patron has connected with your service.

call center—a corporate environment where operators use the telephone and other telecommunications devices to make sales calls, take orders, and provide customer services. This term is increasingly being replaced by contact center.

canned responses—pre-scripted messages that save you typing time in a live virtual reference transaction. Too many canned responses may make an operator seem to not be a live person. Also called scripted messages or pre-formatted responses.

chat—a real-time conversation that occurs by typing over the Internet.

co-browsing—the ability to synch up the user's browser with the librarian's browser so that the user is able to see what the librarian sees, and the user can see what the user sees. Also known as two-way page pushing. In a co-browse session the vendor's server functions as a proxy for an organization's Web site and sits between both the user and librarian's computers and the organization's Web site. All interactions are routed through the proxy, allowing a librarian to share a single image of a personalized Web page that reflects the user's cookie. Problems with co-browsing include security holes and Web sites that actively prevent co-browsing.

contact center—a corporate environment where operators use many telecommunications tools, not just the telephone. Contact centers may be involved in e-mail or e-commerce marketing, as opposed to telemarketing, and they may also coordinate Internet chat sessions. They may be referred to as Web contact centers.

Customer Relationship Management (CRM)—an information industry term for the methodologies, software, and Internet capabilities that help an organization manage customer relationships in an organized way. An organization might develop a database about its customers that describes relationships in detail. Management, salespeople, people providing service, and perhaps the customer could directly access the information, match customer needs with product plans and offerings, remind customers of service requirements, know what other products a customer had purchased, and generally use customers behavior and stated needs and desires to improve products and services.

Erlang C—an algorithm that can be used to predict customer service or reference staffing needs.

face-to-face reference—traditional question answering service of the print-based library.

Linux—an operating system favored by open source programmers.

live virtual reference—real-time human help delivered through the Internet. Also referred to as chat reference, Web-based reference, or live digital reference.

LSSI—Library Systems and Services, one of the dominant providers of live virtual reference software for libraries. LSSI also provides training for librarians and librarian operators who are available to answer overflow and after-hours questions.

MOO—Multiuser object oriented environment. The chat that occurs in an MOO usually occurs between multiple individuals in a room instead of one-to-one.

open source software—software that is free in the sense that users of the software are free to use it, modify it, and redistribute it, as long as the software remains free. Most open source software is distributed under the terms of the GNU General Public License.

page pushing—sending Web page images to a user's browser.

scripted message—see canned responses.

seat—an individual login on a live virtual reference software package. Some vendors charge "by the seat" for additional logins that allow you to have more than one librarian on live virtual reference duty.

synchronous—in real-time, occurring at the same time. A characteristic of live virtual reference.

text-messaging—sending typed messages back and forth in real-time on the Internet.

virtual reference—a simulation of traditional face-to-face desk reference over the Internet or World Wide Web. Virtual reference can be asynchronous, as in e-mail virtual reference, or synchronous, as in live virtual reference.

Voice over IP (VoIP)—voice delivered using the Internet Protocol. Avoids charges of ordinary telephone services. Some believe VoIP will replace chat, but many problems still need to be worked out.

INDEX

1-800-flowers.com, 44
24/7 hours, 11–12, 39, 80, 84
24/7 Reference software product, 106, 108–110

A

Advanced model, 36–40
    evaluation, 153–155
    marketing, 137–139
    software, 105–110
    staffing, 83–86
    training, 125–126
ALA Code of Ethics, 62
Americans with Disabilities Act, 20
AOL Instant Messenger, 14, 31–32, 96–98, 152
Ask Jeeves, 4, 131
Ask-A-Reference, 12

B

Basic model, 29–32
    evaluation, 150–152
    marketing, 134–136
    software, 96–100
    staffing, 79–82
    training, 123–124
Bibliographies, 72–73
Broughton, Kelly, 81

C

Calloway, Michele, 33
Canned responses, 5
    see also Scripted messages
Carterette, Bob, 56, 59
Casson, Rob, 33, 102
Chat, 13, 20, 24–25, 29, 30, 31, 44, 97, 108, 117
    techniques, 119–122
Cleveland Public Library, 56–57, 138
CLEVNET, 11, 20, 58–59
Co-browsing, 6, 19, 56
Coca-Cola, 47
Coffman, Steve, 4, 50, 88, 108
Collaborative Digital Reference Service (CDRS), 39, 156
Collaborative model, 39–43
    evaluation, 155–156
    marketing, 139–141
    software, 110–111
    staffing 86–88
    training, 126–127
Collaborative reference, 12
College of New Jersey, 77
Conferences, 73
Copyright, 26
Cornell University, 84
Corporate model, 44–50
    evaluation, 156
    marketing, 141–143
    software, 111–113
    staffing, 88–89
    training, 128–129
Customer relationship management (CRM), 142

D

DIG-REF listserv, 72, 81
Distance learning, 19
Drew, Bill, 30, 97

E

eGain, 106, 109
E-learning, 128
E-mail reference 10–11, 18–19
Erlang C, 88
Evaluation, 145–157

F

Face-to-face reference, 9–10, 155, 157
Fagan, Jody Condit, 33, 103
Ford, 47
Francoeur, Stephen, 69, 132
Frequently asked questions (FAQs), 4, 47

H

Homegrown model, 32–36

evaluation, 152–153
marketing, 136–137
software, 100–105
staffing, 82
training, 124–125
Homework help, 20
HumanClick, 142

I

Institute of Museum and Library Services, 60
Internet Public Library, 85

K

Keystone Library Network, 155
King County Library, 20
Knowledge base, 155
Kotler, Philip, 133

L

Land O'Lakes, 44
Land's End, 18
Librarian's Index to the Internet, 85, 119
Library Services and Technology Act (LSTA), 39, 60, 140
Library Systems and Services (LSSI), 39, 57, 103, 106–112
Licenses, 26
Lipow, Anne, 13
Listservs, 72
LiveAssistance, 96
LivePerson, 96, 98–100, 110
LiveRef, 68–69
Livereference listserv, 72
Live virtual reference
arguments against, 22–26
arguments for, 17–21
defined 3–4
distinguished from e-mail reference, 3
fear of, 24
names for, 13–14
policies, 61–63, 122–123

technical problems, 25
visual and oral cues, lack of, 119

M

McKiernan, Gerry, 67–69, 73
Marketing, 21, 131–144
advanced model, 137–139
basic model, 134–136
collaborative model, 139–141
corporate model, 141–143
homegrown model, 136–137
Marsteller, Matt, 70–71
Massachusetts Institute of Technology (MIT), 37, 107
Metropolitan Cooperative Library System (MCLS), 40, 92, 108–109, 140
Miami University (Ohio), 33, 102–103
MOO, 13–14
Morris County Library, 20
Morris Messenger, 33, 103
Multitasking, 121

N

Neuhaus, Paul, 70–71, 81
North Carolina State University, 11, 37, 56, 83, 107, 108
Northern Illinois Alliance Library System, 11

O

Open source software, 33, 100, 101, 153
Oracle, 47

P

Page pushing, 6, 19, 56
example of, 40
Policy, 61–63
Print reference materials, 85
Privacy, 62–63, 149, 155
Public Information Kiosk, 138

Q

Q and A Cafe, 40, 140
Q and A NJ, 39, 110–111, 140, 141

R

RAKIM, 102
Reference
    core skills, 118–119
    questions, decreasing number of, 17, 22, 132
    reference interview, 19, 119
    remote, 12
    roving, 99

S

Santa Monica Public Library, 109
Sauers, Michael, 118
Scripted messages, 5, 121
    example of, 45
    see also Canned responses
Sloan, Bernie, 73, 132
Software, 91–113P
South Jersey Regional Library Cooperative (SJRLC), 141
Southern Illinois University, 103–105
Staffing, 22, 79–89
SUNY Morrisville, 30–32, 97
Surveys, 70–72

T

Teaching Librarian, 69–70
Telephone reference, 10
Temple University, 5–8, 19, 56, 58, 64, 77, 101–102, 136
Text messaging, 96
Training, 117–129

U

UCLA, 58
University of Illinois at Urbana-Champaigne, 132, 150
University of Pennsylvania, 84

V

Virtual Reference Desk conference, 71, 73
Voice Over Internet Protocol (VoIP), 25, 93, 112–113
vRep, 48

W

Webhelp, 44, 142
Weingand, Darlene, 133
Wesleyan University, 132
Workload, 22

Y

Yahoo calendar, 127

ABOUT THE AUTHORS

MARC MEOLA is Humanities Librarian at the College of New Jersey. He received his bachelor's degree in philosophy from Rutgers University, a master's degree in library and information science also from Rutgers, and a master's degree in philosophy from Johns Hopkins University. At the College of New Jersey he established an e-mail virtual reference service and is a member of the VALE virtual reference committee, a statewide committee charged with exploring collaborative virtual reference in New Jersey. Together with Sam Stormont, he created a live virtual reference service in 1998. With Stormont he has co-authored a journal article and spoken at various conferences on the topic of live virtual reference.

SAM STORMONT is Digital Reference Services Coordinator and Communications Subject Specialist at Temple University. He holds a bachelor's degree from DePauw University in communications, a master's degree in information science from Drexel University, and a master's in communications from Temple. Before his current appointment, he had the good fortune to be associated with Telebase Systems, a company that pioneered the use of online reference services. He established an e-mail reference service at Temple, and with Marc Meola, launched one of the first live virtual reference services in 1998. He has published several articles and given numerous presentations about live virtual reference.

UMASS Dartmouth

3 2922 00485 227 0

WITHDRAWN

DATE DUE

ILL# 797440		
DUE 08/26/03		
SEP 2 9 2003		

Demco, Inc. 38-293